WINDOWS

OF *Hope*

THANKING
AND TRUSTING
A SOVEREIGN GOD

C. RAMSEY TURPIN

All Scripture is from the Holy Bible, New International Version®, NIV® unless otherwise noted. Copyright ©1973, 1978, 1984, 2011 by Biblica, Inc.® Used by permission. All rights reserved worldwide.

HIS Publishing Group
4301 Wiley Post Road Suite 201D
Addison, TX 75001

Library of Congress Control Number: 2021911074
ISBN: 978-0-9825756-9-7

Printed in the United States of America

Second Edition

HISPUBLISHING
GROUP

Printed in the United States of America
Division of Human Improvement Specialists, llc.
www.hispubg.com | info@hispubg.com

Dedicated to my husband, Fred,
whose love and loyalty were mine
for almost a half century,
even as iron was sharpening iron.

PREFACE

piritual markers on the timeline of a life often coincide with births and deaths, even as far back as the Biblical record of human history. Genesis tells us, "Enoch walked with God when he became the father of Methusalah," and Isaiah wrote, "In the year that King Uzziah died, I saw the Lord...." about his vision and call from God. When my beloved Mother died, I read a quote in a gift book that became a new spiritual marker in my life. A 19th century Christian leader, preacher Charles H. Spurgeon, wrote:

> "Faith goes up the stairs that Love has built and looks out the windows which Hope has opened."

The window Hope opens....a window of Hope! Faith, love, and hope are often intertwined and interconnected in Scripture....the first two combining to produce hope. Not a frivolous or pie-in-the-sky hope, but *a living hope*, a hope based on God's unfailing love and a faith in Jesus, the resurrected Christ. My mind could picture a frail figure with head hanging down, slowly ascending from a drab, dark cellar, up stairs built on the sure foundation of God's love. At the top of the stairs a window has opened, revealing a bright, sunlit vista, renewing heart and hope....as if one has been "rescued from the dominion of darkness." God's words of hope in Scripture could become Windows of Hope to inspire or encourage anyone whose faith is being stretched by life's harsh realities. I determined to collect and reflect on Bible verses about hope....messages from the God of Hope....to meditate on and share as reminders that the true source of hope is found in God alone. To draw hopeless hearts to this true Source became a call, a new spiritual marker on my timeline. I could not know it then, but for almost two decades, I would be the one in constant need of overflowing hope. The verses of hope collection and reflections would become <u>Windows of Hope</u> for my own grieving heart.

Mother's agonizing death from Alzheimer's disease was followed by my father's stroke and his courageous but unsuccessful three-year effort to recover from its effects. Two words described those years: cares and prayers. Then came more tough years. My aging joints required several replacement surgeries, business problems arose, and some valued relationships were fractured. But nothing prepared me for the news that my husband had a metastasized cancer requiring several surgeries, multiple rounds of radiation, weekly infusion therapy, and countless appointments over the next two years, before a heart-breaking pronouncement that his treatment options had run out.

Fatigue, frustration, disappointment and sorrow alternated as the order of the day for those two years. Efforts to be hopeful on my own had to be relinquished to God. But when I did that, His great faithfulness and grace surrounded me as a shield. God's words of hope encouraged and supplied me with "strength for today and bright hope for tomorrow," a hymn phrase from "Great Is Thy Faithfulness." Each morning I would pray, read my Bible and a devotional, and wait to see how God would refresh my hopes for caregiving that day. On all days and in all ways, I was praying for my husband to be a cancer survivor. Rarely did a day go by without some whisper of hope for my heart, encouraging me to focus on God and not on how hopeless the medical situation might seem. The Psalms became my prayer book, and Isaiah, my new best friend.

I clung daily to the words of two particular Scriptures:

> <u>Romans 15:13</u> summarized God's truth regarding hope... *May the God of Hope fill you with all joy and peace as you trust in Him, so that you may overflow with hope by the power of the Holy Spirit.*

My part of that truth was to TRUST God....even if things looked hopeless. God's part was for His Holy Spirit to fill me to overflowing with hope, joy, and peace. Every caregiver needs those gifts to serve and comfort loved ones and others. Further assurance and instruction came in an Old Testament verse:

Isaiah 7:4 Be careful. Keep calm. Do not fear. Do not lose heart.

These words had been given by God to Isaiah to reassure and encourage a king of Judah who was facing powerful enemies. The king chose to ignore them. But thousands of years later, God would use those very words to bring encouragement to me as I faced the enemies of fear, discouragement, and fading hopes. During my husband's brave battle with cancer, I needed daily to <u>be careful</u> and to <u>keep calm</u>....to guard against <u>fear</u>fulness and hopelessness by <u>not losing heart</u>. Only the Lord could make this possible for me.

As I cried out to God, He held my hand, sustained my strength and enabled my energy. He proved the truth of His Word: _His mercies are new every morning,_ regardless of the day's challenges or needs. If at this moment you are desperate for a word of hope, tell your Heavenly Father, your Creator, the God of Hope. Your circumstances have not taken Him by surprise. He knows your questions, your doubts, your fears and failures. The Lord also knows the intent and desire of your heart in seeking the hope He alone can supply. Do not resist or dismiss His outstretched arms. Ask God to help your unbelief and to strengthen your slivers of faith to trust in Him. Meditate on His words of hope, even when love has to make a tearful good-bye. God's comfort and peace whispered reminders to my heart that belonging to Christ Jesus means that good-bye for now is not forever!

My days as a widow began with a personal crisis of confidence. I had been sure of the call to collect Windows of Hope Scriptures, but self-doubt began to nibble away at the idea of sharing this collection. In my season of loss and grieving, I felt totally inadequate to think about inspiring other hearts to trust in God's power to give hope. But God called to mind this verse in I Thessalonians 5:4 KJV: "....faithful is He who calleth you who also will do it." How? The same way the Sovereign God had taught me since childhood days of singing "Jesus Loves Me" and "Jesus Wants Me for a Sunbeam." It was one step at a time....to know and grow in the Scriptures, discovering God's unfailing love, His will, and the wonder of His ways with His creation. His unseen hand is always at work, even when we fail to see or look for the evidence. The privilege of my life was learning and serving in the classes of Bible Study Fellowship International, discovering for myself that the Scriptures are God's truth for every age, stage, season, and need of our lives.

The Bible is not just a random collection of stories, songs, poetry, genealogies, and parables, nor is it just a book of history. It is His story....God's story....His account of the creation of the universe, and His relationship to us and with us. The amazing reality is that the Bible is always true, but ever new. Read it as an invitation to a personal relationship: with God, our Creator and heavenly Father....with His Son, Jesus Christ, our Redeemer from the sins of doing life our own way instead of God's way....with the Holy Spirit as our powerful helper, comforter, and supplier of a living hope. The more I learn from the Scriptures about the character of God, His power and purposes, His holiness and faithfulness, the more I am humbled by His unconditional and unfailing love for me.

The unmistakable Biblical mandate for me became to THANK and TRUST this Sovereign God, whatever was going on in my daily life. Even when things look hopeless, when there appears to be nothing for which to be thankful, I can refocus my heart and mind from troubles and trials to thanks for God's promises to me....promises regarding His presence, His power, His provisions and His protection.

The matter of thanking and trusting God becomes easier the more you do it. Experience with His faithfulness has taught me to put my needs, desires, shortages, failures, mistakes, fears, disappointments, and grief in His hand. I acknowledge my trust by releasing to God's keeping power all of those mounting anxieties. Words from an old hymn sum up the trust admonition: "Trust Him when dark doubts assail thee/ Trust Him when thy strength is small/Trust Him when to simply trust Him/Seems the hardest thing of all."

WINDOWS OF HOPE is a challenge to put the THANK and TRUST dynamic to work today, using God's own words as you talk and pray to Him. Gratitude for His grace helps us stand firm and believe that though we cannot always trace God, we can always trust Him! Make the suggested verses of trust and thanks a foundation for prayers and petitions. Time spent with God in His Word is never wasted. He wants a relationship with you. And as you use His words to confirm your thanks and trust, your heart begins to calm, hope begins to renew, and your wearied soul is refreshed in surprising ways.

The amazing fact about our Sovereign, loving God is that He is always wiser, kinder, and better than we know. He is more willing to give us hope than we are to admit our need for it. He is more willing to show us that *mercy triumphs over judgment* than we are willing to give someone the benefit of the doubt. And He is more willing to extend grace and forgiveness to us than we are to grant either to someone who has wronged us. That's because His ways are higher than our ways. But if His thoughts, revealed in Scripture, can become our thoughts, then our hopes will soar in thankfulness that we can withstand the storms and trials of this life by trusting Him....always acknowledging there are mysteries with God we can never fully explain or understand.

Even as I began to put print on paper, my crisis of confidence about compiling this hope collection was not totally resolved. Along with Scriptures' calls to steadfastness, a reminder to persevere came from an American president, John Quincy Adams: "Duty is ours, results are God's." Trusting the Lord, I continued to go forward. As a former schoolteacher, I knew to anticipate questions or problems that can come up after the introduction of a new concept or challenge. Presenting Windows of Hope was no different. One concern involved a fear of perceived redundancy....the repetition in the Biblical message regarding hope. But if the God who created us knows we learn best by repetition, why should we take offense at frequent re-statements of the same truths? God's words were given to multiple generations and leaders over the centuries as reminders of His faithfulness. Think how many times God says in Scripture, "Do not fear. Do not be afraid. Fear not, I am with you." Yet when life storms hit us and panic starts, are we not grateful that God reminds us again of what He has said to His people over and over? Repetition is an aid to trusting, understanding, and application. (Experienced aviators already know redundancy can be a life-saver!)

Another concern was the many different versions of the Bible available today (translations, paraphrases, and amplifications). The words in one Bible may not match exactly the words in another. Confusion can result. But, amazingly, as if the Scripture verses were glimmering jewels with many facets, reading multiple translations or versions of the same verse reveals an even brighter spectrum of light and meaning than reading only one. More important than which Bible version you use is your belief that the words are from God: true and meant for you, so that you might know His power to bring you life, hope and help whatever your situation. Do not be afraid to underline or write in your Bible. Mark and date verses noting when or how God used the words in your life and heart. The notations become treasured reminders of God's past faithfulness....hope-boosters for the next storm or crisis....or a way to share with another how God's words gave your heart endurance and hope. The God of Hope revives sagging spirits in countless, creative ways. He often uses wise words and examples from other believers to grow us up in Him. Inspiring stories from God's servants of every generation can bless us and be a blessing to pass on. Once again, we learn God is always true to His word, no matter when we need it or read it!

Isaiah is still one of my best friends for inspiration and hope. Words he spoke concerning a personal attribute have become a desire of my heart: *The Sovereign Lord has given me an instructed tongue, to know the word that sustains the weary."* (50:4) My prayer is that each day your weary heart or flagging hope will be encouraged by God's words as you thank and trust Him. Hopelessness comes when we think our situation will never change. But the wonder of God's ways is that He delights to hear our prayer for hope….a living hope that changes the outlook of any heart, transformed by Jesus' presence there.

WINDOWS OF HOPE is offered as a sacrifice of praise to a Sovereign God, the God of Hope, whose unfailing love and faithfulness have held me close with assurance that He is always with me….and that His grace is sufficient for me, even when my heart's deepest prayers would not be answered the way I had hoped. Regardless of your current situation, or the present measure of your Faith, may you climb the stairs Love has built and look out a window Hope has opened….Hope based on the Living Word, Jesus Christ, and on God's written Word in the Bible. Then you will prove the Holy Spirit's power to give you overflowing hope, joy, and peace as you choose each day to trust and thank Him.

Praise be to the God and Father of our Lord Jesus Christ! In his great mercy, he has given us new birth into a living hope through the resurrection of Jesus Christ from the dead...

I Peter 1:3

For centuries philosophers and poets have penned words about hope: "Hope springs eternal..." and "While there is life, there's hope." Perhaps you have even quoted these statements, thinking they were Biblical, not knowing Alexander Pope and Cicero were the sources. Reformer Martin Luther said, "Everything that is done in this world is done in hope." British statesman Benjamin Disreali wisely professed, "I am prepared for the worst, but hope for the best." And from preacher G.K. Chesterton, "Hope is the power of being cheerful in a situation we know to be desperate." Romans 5:5...*hope does not disappoint us.*

Only the living can hope. Our eternal, heavenly Father, the God of Hope, in His mercy, made a living hope possible through faith in His Son, crucified as atonement for our sin, then raised from death to life. Is there anyone who would not choose a living hope over a dying wish?

The certainty of physical death has always been a source of fear, dread, even despair. But thanks be to God for the merciful and loving gift of his Son, by whom we can claim victory over death, our great enemy! So do not ignore or refuse God's gift of salvation and eternal life offered freely to all. Our earthly "living hope" becomes a certain heavenly hope. *Death has been swallowed up in victory* through the risen Lord Jesus Christ. No wonder the Apostle Peter called for praise!!

THANK GOD: John 3:16 ▪ Romans 15:13 ▪ Ephesians 1:18
TRUST GOD: Romans 5:5,8 ▪ I Corinthians 15:54,57 ▪ I John 5:13

Thank God:

John 3:16
For God so loved the world that he gave his one and only Son, that whoever believes in him shall not perish but have eternal life.

Romans 15:13
May the God of hope fill you with all joy and peace as you trust in him, so that you may overflow with hope by the power of the Holy Spirit.

Ephesians 1:18
I pray that the eyes of your heart may be enlightened in order that you may know the hope to which he has called you, the riches of his glorious inheritance in his holy people...

Trust God:

Romans 5:5, 8
And hope does not put us to shame, because God's love has been poured out into our hearts through the Holy Spirit, who has been given to us.

But God demonstrates his own love for us in this: While we were still sinners, Christ died for us.

I Corinthians 15:54, 57
When the perishable has been clothed with the imperishable, and the mortal with immortality, then the saying that is written will come true: "Death has been swallowed up in victory."

But thanks be to God! He gives us the victory through our Lord Jesus Christ.

I John 5:13
I write these things to you who believe in the name of the Son of God so that you may know that you have eternal life.

I rise before dawn and cry for help; I have put my hope in your word.

Psalm 119:147

Reading, knowing, and believing God's word is the pathway to hope, help, and security. The longest Psalm in the Bible focuses on the importance of trusting the truth of God's words in Scripture….believing God for His word and then seeing the results of taking it to heart! When you are in dire need of God's help, open your Bible and read God's words of promise in Psalms. Pray God's words from Scripture back to Him, as if reminding Him of His promises (though He already knows all of them!). Using Scripture in prayer accesses His strength, wisdom, and power to work for your good in whatever has befallen or befuddled you. God is always true to His word. Read it, pray it, and trust Him.

Whether confessing hope in God's words or crying out for strength and help, Psalm 119 brings treasures of faith to heart and mind. The hope factor is a recurring theme. *Remember your word to your servant, for you have given me hope.* [49] *May those who fear you rejoice when they see me, for I have put my hope in your word.* [74] *My soul faints with longing for your salvation, but I have put my hope in your word.* [81] Psalmists and Prophets of the Old Testament kept hopes alive for the coming of a Redeemer. In the fullness of God's timing, Jesus, the living Word, would come. The New Testament reveals His birth, death, resurrection, and ascension….and believers' hopes now extend to the return of Christ to reign on earth in triumphant glory. No matter your need, put your hope in Jesus, God's living Word of salvation and hope for believers yesterday, today, tomorrow, and until His return to reign and rule.

THANK GOD: Psalm 119:89-90 ▪ Psalm 119:105 ▪ Psalm 119:116
TRUST GOD: Psalm 119:11,28 ▪ Psalm 119:143-144 ▪ Acts 1:10-11

Thank God:

Psalm 119:89-90
Your word, Lord, is eternal; it stands firm in the heavens. Your faithful-ness continues through all generations; you established the earth, and it endures.

Psalm 119:105
Your word is a lamp for my feet, a light on my path.

Psalm 119:116
Sustain me, my God, according to your promise, and I will live; do not let my hopes be dashed.

Trust God:

Psalm 119:11, 28
I have hidden your word in my heart that I might not sin against you.

My soul is weary with sorrow; strengthen me according to your word.

Psalm 119:143-144
Trouble and distress have come upon me, but your commands give me delight. Your statutes are always righteous; give me understanding that I may live.

Acts 1:10-11
They were looking intently up into the sky as he was going, when suddenly two men dressed in white stood beside them. "Men of Galilee," they said, "why do you stand here looking into the sky? This same Jesus, who has been taken from you into heaven, will come back in the same way you have seen him go into heaven."

*We have this hope as an anchor
for the soul, firm and secure.*

Hebrews 6:19

When a sea captain wants his ship to remain in place, immoveable even in changing tides and stormy weather, the order is given to cast or drop anchor. The heavy anchor itself does not secure the ship; it is the placement of it against the firm foundation of the ocean floor that stays the vessel. Our 21st century lives, like a ship, need an anchor to keep us from drifting aimlessly about, being tossed back and forth by changing philosophies, by rising and ebbing fortunes, by personal life storms that blow up out of nowhere, by a worldwide pandemic, or by a fear of death as the final victor.

We are all hoping in something or for something. But on what hope do you seek to anchor your life? A bank account? Intelligence and education? Good deeds? Generous philanthropy? A moral life? Your parents' faith? All are possibilities, but the only hope anchor that can withstand all our quandaries, fears, crises and storms is Jesus Christ, our Savior. This hope anchor is secured by His death, resurrection and ascension to the Father, whose trustworthiness is the bedrock holding our life anchor in place. When Christ becomes our firm and secure hope anchor, we learn another casting concept. Our God invites us to cast all our cares and anxieties upon Him because He cares for us. We may not be fishermen like Jesus' friends, but the anchor and casting analogies are vital to every life. Let Jesus be your hope anchor; then begin confidently casting those fears, cares, and anxieties on Him. As our hopeful lives begin to stabilize, let us thank and trust God for His promises of a soul firm and secure!

THANK GOD: Romans 5:5 ▪ Philippians 1:20 ▪ Hebrews 3:16
TRUST GOD: I Peter 5:7 ▪ Psalm 55:22 ▪ I John 3:2-3

Thank God:

Romans 5:5
And hope does not put us to shame, because God's love has been poured out into our hearts through the Holy Spirit, who has been given to us.

Philippians 1:20
I eagerly expect and hope that I will in no way be ashamed, but will have sufficient courage so that now as always Christ will be exalted in my body, whether by life or by death.

Hebrews 3:16
Who were they who heard and rebelled? Were they not all those Moses led out of Egypt?

Trust God:

I Peter 5:7
Cast all your anxiety on him because he cares for you.

Psalm 55:22
Cast your cares on the Lord and he will sustain you; he will never let the righteous be shaken.

I John 3:2-3
Dear friends, now we are children of God, and what we will be has not yet been made known. But we know that when Christ appears, we shall be like him, for we shall see him as he is. All who have this hope in him purify themselves, just as he is pure.

Thou wilt keep him in perfect peace whose mind
is stayed on thee, because he trusts in thee.

Isaiah 26:3 KJV

The terrible twins of terror and tyranny dominate news headlines every day. A background of global insecurity, co-mingled with personal life storms, sets us up for fears and anxieties at every turn. Is peace of mind even possible in today's complicated world? Can we really hope for an end to tyranny and terror? Jesus himself answers that question when He tells his disciples: *In the world you will have trouble, but take heart! I have overcome the world.* (John 16:33)

Finding peace of mind and heart is only possible when our eyes are focused on a Sovereign God. Words of endurance and encouragement from Scripture become our weapons to combat the assault on our faith and peace. When fearful imaginations play mind-games, decide to apply God's word to paralyzing news. Lord, keep my mind stayed on Jesus, the Prince of Peace....our source for that peace that passes understanding.

"If we forget that the newspapers are footnotes to Scripture and not the other way around, we will finally be afraid to get out of bed in the morning." So warned Eugene H. Peterson, best known for The Message, a contemporary rendering of the Biblical texts. Today we seek news through multi-media, but let us not forget to keep God's words of peace, hope, and comfort in our hearts. When the world seems out-of-control, remember that God is not taken by surprise. May we find ourselves "surprised by joy" when we "take heart," believing God concerning His peace and trusting in Jesus, who has overcome the world.

THANK GOD: Psalm 40:1-2 ▪ Isaiah 54:14 ▪ II Thessalonians 3:16
TRUST GOD: Psalm 112:7-8 ▪ Isaiah 43:1-2 ▪ Philippians 4:6-7

Thank God:

Psalm 40:1-2
I waited patiently for the Lord; he turned to me and heard my cry. He lifted me out of the slimy pit, out of the mud and mire; he set my feet on a rock and gave me a firm place to stand.

Isaiah 54:14
In righteousness you will be established: Tyranny will be far from you; you will have nothing to fear. Terror will be far removed; it will not come near you.

II Thessalonians 3:16
Now may the Lord of peace himself give you peace at all times and in every way. The Lord be with all of you.

Trust God:

Psalm 112:7-8
They will have no fear of bad news; their hearts are steadfast, trusting in the Lord. Their hearts are secure, they will have no fear; in the end they will look in triumph on their foes.

Isaiah 43:1-2
But now, this is what the Lord says—he who created you, Jacob, he who formed you, Israel: "Do not fear, for I have redeemed you; I have summoned you by name; you are mine. When you pass through the waters, I will be with you; and when you pass through the rivers, they will not sweep over you. When you walk through the fire, you will not be burned; the flames will not set you ablaze."

Philippians 4:6-7
Do not be anxious about anything, but in every situation, by prayer and petition, with thanksgiving, present your requests to God. And the peace of God, which transcends all understanding, will guard your hearts and your minds in Christ Jesus.

But the eyes of the Lord are on those
who fear him, on those who hope
in his unfailing love.

Psalm 33:18

A "fear of the Lord" phenomenon is frequently mentioned in the Psalms, always closely linking the believer with a privilege or blessing from Him. The "fear" relationship with the Lord is not a scary or paralyzing type of fear but an awesome, respectful reverence for the almighty power and absolute holiness of a Sovereign God. The God-fearing have His eyes upon them, implying His watchful and protective care. Those all-seeing eyes are also *on those who hope in his unfailing love....*as if the next step after fearing God is yearning in hope to know more of the promise of His unending and unfailing love.

A companion verse, Psalm 147:11, further reveals that God has great pleasure in our fearing Him and hoping in His love. *The Lord delights in those who fear him, who put their hope in his mercy. (KJV)* Could there be any more satisfying thought than knowing your Creator takes delight in you? Ask yourself, "Do my words and thoughts honor and reverence God in private and in public? Have I ever thanked Him for His unfailing love and mercy toward me?" If "yes" is your answer, then you fear the Lord, and you are His delight.

The blessing and privilege of fearing God is having His eyes always upon us, being in His sight no matter where we are geographically, physically, emotionally, or spiritually. He sees us, wants His best for us, and offers us the hope of love unfailing and mercy unending. Are you numbered among those who fear the Lord? You are blessed!

THANK GOD: Proverbs 1:7, 9:10 ▪ Psalm 112:1 ▪ Psalm 115:11
TRUST GOD: Deuteronomy 10:12 ▪ Psalm 34:9,11,15 ▪ I Peter 3:12

Thank God:

Proverbs 1:7, 9:10
The fear of the Lord is the beginning of knowledge, but fools despise wisdom and instruction.

The fear of the Lord is the beginning of wisdom, and knowledge of the Holy One is understanding.

Psalm 112:1
Praise the Lord. Blessed are those who fear the Lord, who find great delight in his commands.

Psalm 115:11
You who fear him, trust in the Lord—he is their help and shield.

Trust God:

Deuteronomy 10:12
And now, Israel, what does the Lord your God ask of you but to fear the Lord your God, to walk in obedience to him, to love him, to serve the Lord your God with all your heart and with all your soul...

Psalm 34:9, 11, 15
Fear the Lord, you his holy people, for those who fear him lack nothing.

Come, my children, listen to me; I will teach you the fear of the Lord.

The eyes of the Lord are on the righteous, and his ears are attentive to their cry.

I Peter 3:12
For the eyes of the Lord are on the righteous and his ears are attentive to their prayer, but the face of the Lord is against those who do evil.

Give thanks to the Lord, for He is good.
His love endures forever.

Psalm 136:1

With every New Year, I choose a word or an attribute for the Lord to develop more fully in my life that year. One year my choice was "gratitude," as I began to make "Thanking and Trusting a Sovereign God" a theme song of my heart. I wanted to grow in expressing my gratitude to the Lord, easily, automatically and prayerfully: "Oh, gracious God, You have <u>sought</u> me from my youth and blessed me in every age, stage, and season of my life. You have <u>bought</u> me eternal life by the redeeming blood of Jesus, your Son. You have <u>brought</u> me to a place of trust in the truth of your Word. You have <u>taught</u> me to seek your kingdom and your wisdom, while trying to renounce my own self-sovereignty, self-centeredness and self-indulgence.

"You have <u>fought</u> for me against fears, foes, and failures, working behind the scenes on my behalf. The battle is not mine, but Thine! You have <u>caught</u> all my cares cast on Thee, working all things for good. You have <u>wrought</u> countless miracles and wonders in my life and have been my strength on every journey, chosen or unchosen. So gratitude <u>ought</u> to be woven throughout my life's tapestry, even with those dark or black threads that make the end design more clear and colorful.

"My desire, Lord, is to show you more gratitude by *the words of my mouth and the meditations of my heart*, by generosity from my hand, and by graciousness in relationships with others....always thanking you for your love and goodness to me, in the holy name of Jesus." Amen.

THANK GOD: Job 9:10 ▪ John 3:16 ▪ Romans 8:28
TRUST GOD: II Chronicles 20:15 ▪ Psalm 19:14 ▪ I Peter 5:7

Thank God:

Job 9:10
He performs wonders that cannot be fathomed, miracles that cannot be counted.

John 3:16
For God so loved the world that he gave his one and only Son, that whoever believes in him shall not perish but have eternal life.

Romans 8:28
And we know that in all things God works for the good of those who love him, who have been called according to his purpose.

Trust God:

II Chronicles 20:15
He said: "Listen, King Jehoshaphat and all who live in Judah and Jerusalem! This is what the Lord says to you: 'Do not be afraid or discouraged because of this vast army. For the battle is not yours, but God's.'"

Psalm 19:14
May these words of my mouth and this meditation of my heart be pleasing in your sight, Lord, my Rock and my Redeemer.

I Peter 5:7
Cast all your anxiety on him because he cares for you.

*...for the Lord is the God who knows, and
by Him deeds are weighed.*

I Samuel 2:3

If you have not yet learned to trust the Lord, His all-knowing attribute seems incomprehensible or very scary. How could He possibly know my thoughts and motives, my hopes and dreams, my faults and failures? I want to keep those to myself! Yet the Scriptures and experience teach us He knows everything about us, loves us still, and has plans for our good, even if current circumstances seem anything but favorable. Centuries of believers have thankfully trusted and treasured Him as "the God who knows." No need to pretend or perform.

Hannah trusted this "God who knows" with her son, Samuel, as she consecrated him to a lifetime in His service. At the dedication of the Temple in Jerusalem, Solomon prayed for God to intervene and forgive, saying, "You alone know every human heart." The prophet Ezekiel, brought by the Spirit to a valley full of dry bones, was asked, "Son of man, can these bones live?" His answer, "O Sovereign Lord, you alone know." Job, in his misery of loss, disease, and his friends' futile analyses, spoke a credo for all who endure prolonged suffering: "But <u>He knows</u> the way that I take; when he has tested me, I shall come forth as gold."

Nothing in all of creation is hidden from God's sight. For better or worse, *everything is laid bare before the eyes of Him to whom we must give an account.* He knows our intentions when we are misjudged, maligned unfairly, or make innocent mistakes. He knows an obedient heart trying to please Him. What a comfort to know God's omniscience!

THANK GOD: Psalm 44:21 ▪ Psalm 139:1-3 ▪ Ezekiel 37:2-3
TRUST GOD: Job 23:10 ▪ I Kings 8:39 ▪ Hebrews 4:13

Thank God:

Psalm 44:21
...would not God have discovered it, since he knows the secrets of the heart?

Psalm 139:1-3
You have searched me, Lord, and you know me. You know when I sit and when I rise; you perceive my thoughts from afar. You discern my going out and my lying down; you are familiar with all my ways.

Ezekiel 37:2-3
He led me back and forth among them, and I saw a great many bones on the floor of the valley, bones that were very dry. He asked me, "Son of man, can these bones live?" I said, "Sovereign Lord, you alone know."

Trust God:

Job 23:10
But he knows the way that I take; when he has tested me, I will come forth as gold.

I Kings 8:39
...then hear from heaven, your dwelling place. Forgive and act; deal with everyone according to all they do, since you know their hearts (for you alone know every human heart)...

Hebrews 4:13
Nothing in all creation is hidden from God's sight. Everything is uncovered and laid bare before the eyes of him to whom we must give account.

The Lord, the Lord, is my strength and
my song; He has become my salvation.

Exodus 15:2 Psalm 118:14 Isaiah 12:2

Moses' song of triumph resounds in both Psalms and Isaiah. Repetition of this timeless truth about our Lord urges us to consider Him our source of strength and the reason for our song. You are in good company if the Lord is your strength, your song, and your salvation.

Readers of the Psalms discover that one of the most frequent prayers of God's people is for strength, His strength. The supernatural power of God is the best resource we have to overcome our weakness when we are facing a difficult task or need to stand firm in our faith against an adversary without fainting or failing, persevere one more day in exhausting combat, or make the final ascent up a towering peak. When the work is accomplished, when the victory is won, then we truly can say, "The Lord is my strength." God grants His strength most notably to those who readily admit to Him their weakness and need!

In thankfulness for God-given strength, give Him glory and praise. Nothing speaks gratitude or joy faster than a song of triumph sung to Him and for Him, as Moses sang after the Hebrews' escape across the Red Sea. God had parted the waters; they safely crossed to the other side. God's salvation and deliverance were the reason for the song. Today, God's salvation is through His Son, who delivers and strengthens us. May we give joyous testimony about the Lord being our Savior and our strength....as He creates in us a heart that bursts into song, thankful for Jesus' love and grace as we receive and trust in Him.

THANK GOD: Psalm 28:6-9 ▪ Psalm 96:1-3 ▪ Philippians 4:13
TRUST GOD: I Chronicles 16:9-11 ▪ Psalm 18:1-2 ▪ Habakkuk 3:19

Thank God:

Psalm 28:6-9
Praise be to the Lord, for he has heard my cry for mercy. The Lord is my strength and my shield; my heart trusts in him, and he helps me. My heart leaps for joy, and with my song I praise him. The Lord is the strength of his people, a fortress of salvation for his anointed one. Save your people and bless your inheritance; be their shepherd and carry them forever.

Psalm 96:1-3
Sing to the Lord a new song; sing to the Lord, all the earth. Sing to the Lord, praise his name; proclaim his salvation day after day. Declare his glory among the nations, his marvelous deeds among all peoples.

Philippians 4:13
I can do all things through him who gives me strength.

Trust God:

I Chronicles 16:9-11
Sing to him, sing praise to him; tell of all his wonderful acts. Glory in his holy name; let the hearts of those who seek the Lord rejoice. Look to the Lord and his strength; seek his face always.

Psalm 18:1-2
I love you, Lord, my strength. The Lord is my rock, my fortress and my deliverer; my God is my rock, in whom I take refuge, my shield and the horn of my salvation, my stronghold.

Habakkuk 3:19
The Sovereign Lord is my strength; he makes my feet like the feet of a deer, he enables me to tread on the heights.

Go in the strength you have....
Am I not sending you?

Judges 6:14

Has God ever asked you to do a specific task or to assume a leadership role that seems impossible to you? Do you offer excuses, questions, and disclaimers protesting your lack of ability and qualifications? If so, you can identify with both Moses and Gideon, who were very reluctant leaders when God called them to be deliverers.

While tending sheep, Moses heard God call his name from a flaming bush, enlisting him to go to Pharaoh to bring His people out of Egypt. Moses immediately resisted with excuses: Who am I? Suppose they ask who sent me? What if they do not believe me? I am slow of speech, not eloquent. Measuring our abilities against God's challenge is scary! But we <u>now</u> know the phenomenal signs and wonders God did through his servant Moses when he reluctantly obeyed the Lord's call.

Gideon's call from God to deliver Israel from the Midianites came via His angel. God promised His presence, but Gideon questioned if God was with them, why had Israel fallen into such a predicament in the first place? He made excuses about his clan being weak and his being the youngest in his family. Sound familiar? Gideon even proposed several tests for proof of God's power on his behalf. (Judges 6:36-40) The Lord's indulgence of Gideon's requests attests to His great forbearance with His chosen people. But we <u>now</u> know Gideon's pared down forces won an amazing victory for the Lord. So stop resisting a call from God, and "Go in the strength that you have." If God is sending you, He is and will be with you, and His strength and strategy will lead to victory.

THANK GOD: Exodus 15:13 ▪ Psalm 18:30-32 ▪ Judges 6:12-13,16-17
TRUST GOD: Psalm 28:7-8 ▪ Psalm 60:11-12 ▪ Isaiah 41:10, 55:6

Thank God:

Exodus 15:13
In your unfailing love you will lead the people you have redeemed. In your strength you will guide them to your holy dwelling.

Psalm 18:30-32
As for God, his way is perfect: The Lord's word is flawless; he shields all who take refuge in him. For who is God besides the Lord? And who is the Rock except our God? It is God who arms me with strength and keeps my way secure.

Judges 6:12-13, 16-17
When the angel of the Lord appeared to Gideon, he said, "The Lord is with you, mighty warrior." "Pardon me, my lord," Gideon replied, "but if the Lord is with us, why has all this happened to us? Where are all his wonders that our ancestors told us about when they said, 'Did not the Lord bring us up out of Egypt?' But now the Lord has abandoned us and given us into the hand of Midian."

The Lord answered, "I will be with you, and you will strike down all the Midianites, leaving none alive." Gideon replied, "If now I have found favor in your eyes, give me a sign that it is really you talking to me."

Trust God:

Psalm 28:7-8
The Lord is my strength and my shield; my heart trusts in him, and he helps me....The Lord is the strength of his people, a fortress of salvation for his anointed one.

Psalm 60:11-12
Give us aid against the enemy, for human help is worthless. With God we will gain the victory, and he will trample down our enemies.

Isaiah 41:10, 55:6
So do not fear, for I am with you; do not be dismayed, for I am your God. I will strengthen you and help you; I will uphold you with my righteous right hand.

Seek the Lord while he may be found; call on him while he is near.

*And God is able to make all
grace abound toward you,
so that in all things, at all times, having all that
you need, you may abound in every good work.*

II Corinthians 9:8

God's character is marked by His great generosity. The promises of this verse confirm our God is never stingy, nor does He ever sow sparingly, only generously. He is so gracious and so generous with His grace that we need not be overwhelmed by any challenge life presents or any call He gives us. Just look at "all" the ways He has listed for building our confidence in Him, in His abounding and enabling grace, whatever our circumstance or situation.

God is able to make all grace abound toward us....not a trickle-down grace, but an overflowing of His grace on those who are trusting in Him. And why does He lavish this gift on us? "So that in all things" (academic studies, marriage, parenting, professional or vocational jobs, charity or social work, philanthropy, or special assignment from the Lord), "at all times" (day or night, in every season of the year and each season of our lives), "having all that you need" (time, wisdom, resources, strength, perseverance, guidance, discernment....and the fruit of His Spirit), "you will abound in every good work" (the many ways we are called to love and serve the Lord and others). All grace in all things, at all times, in the face of all needs....so that we can abound in every good work. What a hope-booster this verse is! What a perfect way to pray: asking God for this abounding and inclusive grace! Rejoice in His power to enable and equip us for whatever He has called our hearts to do or be for Him. May we do it graciously and generously for His name's sake!

THANK GOD: Galatians 5:22 ▪ Philippians 4:19 ▪ John 1:16-17
TRUST GOD: II Corinthians 12:9 ▪ Hebrews 4:16 ▪ Colossians 4:6

Thank God:

Galatians 5:22
But the fruit of the Spirit is love, joy, peace, forbearance, kindness, goodness, faithfulness, gentleness and self-control.

Philippians 4:19
And my God will meet all your needs according to the riches of his glory in Christ Jesus.

John 1:16-17
Out of his fullness we have all received grace in place of grace already given. For the law was given through Moses; grace and truth came through Jesus Christ.

Trust God:

II Corinthians 12:9
But he said to me, "My grace is sufficient for you, for my power is made perfect in weakness." Therefore I will boast all the more gladly about my weaknesses, so that Christ's power may rest on me.

Hebrews 4:16
Let us then approach God's throne of grace with confidence, so that we may receive mercy and find grace to help us in our time of need.

Colossians 4:6
Let your conversation be always full of grace, seasoned with salt, so that you may know how to answer everyone.

Let us hold unswervingly to the hope we profess, for He who promised is faithful.

Hebrews 10:23

"When you get a promise from God, it is worth just as much as fulfillment..." So spoke an unknown but wise believer. What are we to do when the fulfillment is not forthcoming or seems long overdue? The Bible challenges us to answer that question in a variety of ways:

Hold on to hope; do not shrink back; wait patiently for the Lord.... He is there, He cares, He hears your prayers. He even provides a role model. By faith, Abraham believed God for His promise to make him a Father of Nations, but by old age, he and his wife did not even have a child. Yet *against all hope, Abraham in hope believed....he did not waver through unbelief regarding the promise of God, but was strengthened in his faith and gave glory to God, being fully persuaded that God had power to do what he had promised.* (Romans 4:20-21) And Isaac, his son, was born.

Trusting the power and goodness of a Sovereign God means leaving to Him the best answer to our hopeful prayers....yes, no, or wait. A wait is not necessarily a denial, but sometimes a "wait" answer could even mean fulfillment will not happen in our lifetime. Yet II Corinthians 1:2 assures believers that *all the promises of God in Christ are Yea and Amen.* Fulfillment of a Biblical promise from God happens in His perfect timing.

God's faithfulness to His promises and our unswerving hope in them provide a delicate balance. How and when are entirely up to God. Our part is to hope without doubting God's word or His power to bring it to pass. Our good and His glory is always the result. Hallelujah!!

THANK GOD: Romans 4:18-19 ▪ I Corinthians 1:9 ▪ Hebrews 11:11-12
TRUST GOD: Psalm 27:13-14 ▪ Luke 18:1 ▪ Romans 12:12

Thank God:

Romans 4:18-19
Against all hope, Abraham in hope believed and so became the father of many nations, just as it had been said to him, "So shall your offspring be." Without weakening in his faith, he faced the fact that his body was as good as dead—since he was about a hundred years old—and that Sarah's womb was also dead.

I Corinthians 1:9
God is faithful, who has called you into fellowship with his Son, Jesus Christ our Lord.

Hebrews 11:11-12
And by faith even Sarah, who was past childbearing age, was enabled to bear children because she considered him faithful who had made the promise. And so from this one man, and he as good as dead, came descendants as numerous as the stars in the sky and as countless as the sand on the seashore.

Trust God:

Psalm 27:13-14
I remain confident of this: I will see the goodness of the Lord in the land of the living. Wait for the Lord; be strong and take heart and wait for the Lord.

Luke 18:1
Then Jesus told his disciples a parable to show them that they should always pray and not give up.

Romans 12:12
Be joyful in hope, patient in affliction, faithful in prayer.

The eternal God is your refuge and underneath are the everlasting arms.

Deuteronomy 33:27

Perhaps from birth you have been daring and fearless. If so, you have no idea what born "scaredy-cats" go through when faced with the challenge to dare and triumph instead of sitting fearfully on the sidelines. Whether it is flying on a plane, traversing a bridge swinging a quarter of a mile above a river, going on a famous wild ride at an amusement park, or riding a chair-lift to the top of a towering peak....more than just hesitation is usually involved. Today's Scripture is a game-changer for anyone hoping for new courage and self-confidence.

Rest your mind on the phrase "underneath are the everlasting arms." Picture strong arms upholding a plane, providing a safety net, or securing suspension cables. Amazingly, when the adventure is over, a new sense of triumph increases our boldness. A perspective change exercises our bravery muscles. With lightness and levity, I can now say to myself when next facing a scary, new challenge, "I've survived rough flights, made it across the Vancouver's Capilano Suspension Bridge, plunged from the Tower of Terror, and been chair-lifted to an Olympic mountain top....I can do this!" Past courage always inspires! Trust God! He is our forever refuge, in adventure or unexpected crisis.

God's word never promotes recklessness, but He is constantly saying not to fear or be afraid. Knowing Him and trusting His word is the key....then thanking Him for His everlasting arms beneath us.

THANK GOD: Joshua 1:9 ▪ Psalm 37:23-24 ▪ II Timothy 1:7
TRUST GOD: Deuteronomy 31:6 ▪ Psalm 94:18-19 ▪ Jeremiah 17:7

Thank God:

Joshua 1:9
Have I not commanded you? Be strong and courageous. Do not be afraid; do not be discouraged, for the Lord your God will be with you wherever you go.

Psalm 37:23-24
The Lord makes firm the steps of the one who delights in him.

II Timothy 1:7
For the Spirit God gave us does not make us timid, but gives us power, love and self-discipline.

Trust God:

Deuteronomy 31:6
Be strong and courageous. Do not be afraid or terrified because of them, for the Lord your God goes with you; he will never leave you nor forsake you.

Psalm 94:18-19
When I said, "My foot is slipping," your unfailing love, Lord, supported me. When anxiety was great within me, your consolation brought me joy.

Jeremiah 17:7
But blessed is the one who trusts in the Lord, whose confidence is in him.

Therefore we do not lose heart. Though
outwardly we are wasting away,
yet inwardly we are
being renewed day by day.

II Corinthians 4:16

Have you ever felt like you were wasting away, perhaps from the hardship of illness or its treatment, from the fatigue and stress of constant caregiving, from the anxious weariness of combat's mortal dangers? God's offer of renewal in the midst of pain or hardship is not found in what we see each day, but what is unseen to the naked eye. *We live by faith, not by sight.* By faith, Moses *persevered because He saw Him who is invisible.*....a model of hope for our lives. We may only be able to see problems, but the Spirit of God can bring to mind Scripture's powerful words of strength, refuge, and protection only He can provide.

Losing heart and hope easily happens in the face of overwhelming struggles. Depending only on our own strength and determination is not a recipe for renewal. Yet dependency on a Sovereign God, whom we cannot see, challenges our desire to be firmly in control of our lives. But the Lord seeks hearts who in humility confess fears, admit weariness, and plead ignorance about how to endure and persevere. Seek His renewal and refreshment in humility and hope....He cares for you!

During the last year of my husband's life, I found God's mercy and faithfulness renewing me each morning. I would rush to my study table to see how God would encourage me once more from His words in the Bible. He never failed me. The Psalms were my prayer book; the prophets my encouragers. In casting my cares on God, I found His strength in my weakness, and His power sustained my energy and love.

THANK GOD: Lamentations 3:22-23 ▪ Hebrews 11:6,27 ▪ I Peter 5:6-7
TRUST GOD: Isaiah 40:28-29 ▪ II Corinthians 5:7 ▪ Hebrews 10:35-36

Thank God:

Lamentations 3:22-23
Because of the Lord's great love we are not consumed, for his compassions never fail. They are new every morning; great is your faithfulness.

Hebrews 11:6, 27
And without faith it is impossible to please God, because anyone who comes to him must believe that he exists and that he rewards those who earnestly seek him.

By faith he left Egypt, not fearing the king's anger; he persevered because he saw him who is invisible.

I Peter 5:6-7
Humble yourselves, therefore, under God's mighty hand, that he may lift you up in due time. Cast all your anxiety on him because he cares for you.

Trust God:

Isaiah 40:28-29
Do you not know? Have you not heard? The Lord is the everlasting God, the Creator of the ends of the earth. He will not grow tired or weary, and his understanding no one can fathom. He gives strength to the weary and increases the power of the weak.

II Corinthians 5:7
For we live by faith, not by sight.

Hebrews 10:35-36
So do not throw away your confidence; it will be richly rewarded. You need to persevere so that when you have done the will of God, you will receive what he has promised.

*For you have been my hope, O Sovereign
Lord, my confidence since my youth.*

Psalm 71:5

Preserving the strength, vigor and confidence of youth is full-time work for anyone facing the ageing process. Fitness training, facelifts, and nutritional supplements all attempt to stop the ageing clock. Perhaps a check on our relationship with God should have an equal time focus, whether we have been blessed to know Him from our youth or are just now beginning to seek His face as ageing becomes a reality.

Psalm 71 is the life-review of an ageing child of God....an honest, vulnerable, yet realistic conversation with the Lord. Almost every verse could become either a prayer for help or a praise for God's faithfulness. *Rescue me and deliver me...*[v2] *Be my rock of refuge to which I can always go...*[v3] *Do not cast me away when I am old, or forsake me when my strength is gone...*[v9] Shame, evil, cruelty, scorn, despair, dreads and fears have all been personally experienced by this Psalmist, maybe by you, too....but a powerful change of perspective comes with the declaration: *But as for me, I will always have hope; I will praise you more and more...*[v14]

"Even when I am old and gray, do not forsake me, O God, till I declare your power to the next generation...[v18] A restored confidence, full of hope, prompts a petition for a witness even to the next generation, proclaiming God's attributes: His righteousness, His powers of redemption, renewal, and restoration. So, confident in God's sovereignty and faithfulness, we can face ageing with hope, knowing He will continue to help us and even use us for His glory.

THANK GOD: Psalm 27:13 ▪ Psalm 71:17, 19 ▪ Psalm 73:28
TRUST GOD: Psalm 46:1 ▪ Jeremiah 17:7 ▪ Nahum 1:7

Thank God:

Psalm 27:13
I remain confident of this: I will see the goodness of the Lord in the land of the living.

Psalm 71:17, 19
Since my youth, God, you have taught me, and to this day I declare your marvelous deeds.

Your righteousness, God, reaches to the heavens, you who have done great things. Who is like you, God?

Psalm 73:28
But as for me, it is good to be near God. I have made the Sovereign Lord my refuge; I will tell of all your deeds.

Trust God:

Psalm 46:1
God is our refuge and strength, an ever-present help in trouble.

Jeremiah 17:7
But blessed is the one who trusts in the Lord, whose confidence is in him.

Nahum 1:7
The Lord is good, a refuge in times of trouble. He cares for those who trust in him...

*Thy word is a lamp to my feet and
a light to my path.*

Psalm 119:105

A walker in dark woods of unknown terrain can have no more valuable possession than a bright lantern or light. Without it, dangers abound: stumbling, falling, bumping headlong into a tree or bramble bush, stepping into a hole or off a cliff. Long before athletic shoes had twinkle lights or cellphone lights were available, the Psalmist knew that God's words are a lamplight when life takes us into unfamiliar territory.

Christmas, 1939, on the eve of World War II, King George VI of England sought to encourage his troubled people. He acknowledged the dire prospects facing his nation and Western civilization, but he challenged them to be undaunted. He quoted a poem by Minnie Haskins, given to him by his daughter, Princess Elizabeth: "I said to the man who stood at the Gate of the Year, 'Give me a light that I may tread safely into the unknown.' And he replied, 'Go out into the darkness, and put your hand into the Hand of God. That shall be to you better than a light and safer than a known way.'" * Better than a light because Jesus is the Light of the World; safer than a known way because Jesus is The Way. King George finished his address by saying, "May that Almighty Hand guide and uphold us all." England held that Hand for five more years.

If you are at the edge of darkness, journeying an unknown way, rely on Jesus. Put your hand in His, and go forth confidently. For the light of God's Word is better than a searchlight and safer than a mapped way.

THANK GOD: Luke 1:78-79 ▪ John 8:12 ▪ John 14:6
TRUST GOD: Psalm 25:4-5 ▪ Isaiah 9:2 ▪ Isaiah 42:16

* Warren, James I., <u>Thoughts from a Sacred Place</u>, First Methodist Church, Waynesville, N.C., pp. 24-25.

Thank God:

Luke 1:78-79

...because of the tender mercy of our God, by which the rising sun will come to us from heaven to shine on those living in darkness and in the shadow of death, to guide our feet into the path of peace.

John 8:12

When Jesus spoke again to the people, he said, "I am the light of the world. Whoever follows me will never walk in darkness, but will have the light of life."

John 14:6

Jesus answered, "I am the way and the truth and the life. No one comes to the Father except through me."

Trust God:

Psalm 25:4-5

Show me your ways, Lord, teach me your paths. Guide me in your truth and teach me, for you are God my Savior, and my hope is in you all day long.

Isaiah 9:2

The people walking in darkness have seen a great light; on those living in the land of deep darkness a light has dawned.

Isaiah 42:16

I will lead the blind by ways they have not known, along unfamiliar paths I will guide them; I will turn the darkness into light before them and make the rough places smooth. These are the things I will do; I will not forsake them.

Be at rest once more, O my soul, for
the Lord has been good to you.

Psalm 116:7

In a moment of crisis, sometimes God's peace seems to be on alternating current rather than a steady, stable flow. When we know Jesus, the Prince of Peace, then the Peace of God should permeate our lives. But that does not mean we are forever immune to anxiety or fear. When bad news or personal unrest occupies our minds, we forget about God's past faithfulness when *He heard my cry for mercy* (Ps. 28:6) and *delivered my soul from death, my feet from stumbling.* (Ps. 56:13) How soon we can lose track of the goodness of God! But if I will quickly turn to my personal journal, or dated notes in the margins of my Bible, and review Scripture related to hope, trust, or deliverance, then before long my self-talk will tell my soul to be still and be at rest once more. God has proven over and over again that He is gracious and full of compassion, a very present help in every kind of trouble.

A sense of restless desperation brings us to our knees to confess our need for greater trust in God's goodness to override our present fears and panic. "Oh, Lord, in the middle of this muddle, let me recall your past goodness, when you have lifted me up from being flat on the mat to swinging in the hammock of your love." Whether you feel defeated by some professional problem, a domestic calamity, or a relationship breakdown or betrayal, always apply for God's goodness to prevail by thanking Him that His unseen hand can work in any distress or disappointment....till rest once more returns to your soul.

THANK GOD: Psalm 116:5-6 ▪ Psalm 143:1 ▪ Philippians 4:7
TRUST GOD: Psalm 31:19 ▪ Psalm 46:1-2 ▪ Isaiah 26:3

Thank God:

Psalm 116:5-6
The Lord is gracious and righteous; our God is full of compassion. The Lord protects the unwary; when I was brought low, he saved me.

Psalm 143:1
Lord, hear my prayer, listen to my cry for mercy; in your faithfulness and righteousness come to my relief.

Philippians 4:7
And the peace of God, which transcends all understanding, will guard your hearts and your minds in Christ Jesus.

Trust God:

Psalm 31:19
How abundant are the good things that you have stored up for those who fear you, that you bestow in the sight of all, on those who take refuge in you.

Psalm 46:1-2
God is our refuge and strength, an ever-present help in trouble. Therefore we will not fear, though the earth give way and the mountains fall into the heart of the sea.

Isaiah 26:3
You will keep in perfect peace those whose minds are steadfast, because they trust in you.

The Lord is good, a stronghold in the day
of trouble; he knoweth them that trust in him.

Nahum 1:7 KJV

When the Lord announces judgment on His foes, inserted in the message of their coming doom is a nugget of encouragement for His own people. He will care for them even as the whirlwind of war engulfs the land. God knows those who trust in Him. The safest place of refuge will be God Himself, surrounding them as a mighty fortress. Nahum called the Lord good, a stronghold, as he prophesied God's judgment on Israel's enemy, Assyria, who had already captured half of Israel's territory.

Where do you seek refuge, a retreat from life's battlefields: earning a living, keeping a family together, caring for dying loved ones, soldiering in a foxhole or war-torn field? Seek a place to read God's word, pray for His wisdom, pour out your heart to Him....a quiet corner, a favorite chair, a lonely barrack. No matter the place, it is the Lord Himself who is your stronghold in troubled times. Trust Him, thank Him for His word in Nahum that He is a safe and strong, caring refuge.

One evening at a large picnic, I met a man named Nahum....a soft-spoken, gentle man, helping with food service. I asked him if he knew Nahum 1:7. He smiled and said he had clung to that verse when two of his sons were born deaf and mute. God became his stronghold, his caring refuge in his days of trouble. He knew this man was trusting in Him for the parenting of these boys, who today have jobs in their community. God honored His word in this father's life, and He will do so in yours.

THANK GOD: Deuteronomy 33:27 ▪ II Samuel 22:3 ▪ Proverbs 3:5-6
TRUST GOD: Psalm 46:1-2 ▪ Psalm 91:2,15 ▪ Psalm 143:8

Thank God:

Deuteronomy 33:27
The eternal God is your refuge, and underneath are the everlasting arms. He will drive out your enemies before you, saying, "Destroy them!"

II Samuel 22:3
...my God is my rock, in whom I take refuge, my shield and the horn of my salvation. He is my stronghold, my refuge and my savior—from violent people you save me.

Proverbs 3:5-6
Trust in the Lord with all your heart and lean not on your own understanding; in all your ways acknowledge him and he will make your paths straight.

Trust God:

Psalm 46:1-2
God is our refuge and strength, an ever-present help in trouble. Therefore we will not fear, though the earth give way and the mountains fall into the heart of the sea...

Psalm 91:2, 15
I will say of the Lord, "He is my refuge and my fortress, my God, in whom I trust."

He will call on me, and I will answer him; I will be with him in trouble, I will deliver him and honor him.

Psalm 143:8
Let the morning bring me word of your unfailing love, for I have put my trust in you. Show me the way I should go, for to you I entrust my life.

A cheerful heart is good medicine.

Proverbs 17:22

Above all else, guard your heart, for it is the wellspring of life. Not just a source of oxygenated blood for our physical health, the believer's heart can also issue streams of living water from within to nourish the spirit of another. (John 7:38) Heart conditions affect overall health. Scripture presents this concept about ten centuries before Christ, but not until the 1970s did medical scientists begin to concur that there actually is a case to be made for laughter and cheer in the promotion of good health, healing, and pain management. A new science was born out of this interest: psychoneuroimmunology. Thoughts, feelings, and attitudes can affect brain chemicals that fight disease. Heart medicines do what they can, but a joyful, cheerful heart can be like medicine to one longing for health and hope. God's wisdom of the ages discovered and applied can make a big difference in our lives!

Many older adults would agree the latter years are not always the golden ones. Aches, pains, syndromes, anxiety, and depression can routinely plague the body and mind. Ever thought about sharing your cheerful heart with someone you know to be feeling low? One day after hearing a hilarious anecdote about age ailments, I took a small vase of colorful snapdragons to a downcast, older friend. Attached to the bouquet was a notecard that read, "Welcome to the 'snapdragon' season of your life….something has snapped, and the rest is dragging." It was a transforming moment of laughter and cheer….good medicine!

THANK GOD: Psalm 139:14 ▪ Proverbs 15:13,15,30 ▪ Proverbs 27:9
TRUST GOD: Proverbs 12:25 ▪ Proverbs 4:23 ▪ Philippians 4:6-7

Thank God:

Psalm 139:14
I praise you because I am fearfully and wonderfully made; your works are wonderful, I know that full well.

Proverbs 15:13, 15, 30
A happy heart makes the face cheerful, but heartache crushes the spirit.

All the days of the oppressed are wretched, but the cheerful heart has a continual feast.

Light in a messenger's eyes brings joy to the heart, and good news gives health to the bones.

Proverbs 27:9
Perfume and incense bring joy to the heart, and the pleasantness of a friend springs from their heartfelt advice.

Trust God:

Proverbs 12:25
Anxiety weighs down the heart, but a kind word cheers it up.

Proverbs 4:23
Above all else, guard your heart, for everything you do flows from it.

Philippians 4:6-7
Do not be anxious about anything, but in every situation, by prayer and petition, with thanksgiving, present your requests to God. And the peace of God, which transcends all understanding, will guard your hearts and your minds in Christ Jesus.

The Sovereign Lord has given me an instructed tongue, to know the word that sustains the weary.

Isaiah 50: 4

If ever you were a hopeful cheerleader-want-to-be, you are familiar with this drill: Learn a routine, a chant, a team cheer. Practice daily with every bit of athleticism, flexibility, and personality you can muster. Acquire for try-outs a suitable outfit. But in spite of all your time, efforts, emotional and physical energy, the outcome is a huge disappointment when the judges fail to select you.

Unlikely as it seems, a losing effort can become a personal teacher. Often we learn more from defeat than from winning. Empathy comes quickly when another experiences a defeat or rejection. Humility is learned when friends tell you how are sorry they are, and you can smile graciously. The Lord may show you in later life that your hopes (like mine) of being a cheerleader were not misplaced. It was simply not God's timing to use you on the football field or the basketball court, but later on in the lives of others….cheering and encouraging them with God's words of comfort and hope. Assurances of God's faithfulness and love can sustain those wearied, not from sports, but from life….health failures, broken family relationships, business or financial troubles.

Who but God could redeem what seemed like a past exercise in futility? Yet in His economy, no challenge we give our best to is ever wasted. God is a Redeemer of our defeats and futile efforts. He can use them for a later, greater purpose than we could ever imagine! He may be calling you to sustain the weary with a word of hope from Him.

THANK GOD: Psalm 31:7 ▪ Psalm 34:8,18 ▪ Isaiah 46:4
TRUST GOD: Proverbs 3:5-6 ▪ Psalm 33:20-22 ▪ Job 23:10

Thank God:

Psalm 31:7
I will be glad and rejoice in your love, for you saw my affliction and knew the anguish of my soul.

Psalm 34:8, 18
Taste and see that the Lord is good; blessed is the one who takes refuge in him.

The Lord is close to the brokenhearted and saves those who are crushed in spirit.

Isaiah 46:4
Even to your old age and gray hairs I am he, I am he who will sustain you. I have made you and I will carry you; I will sustain you and I will rescue you.

Trust God:

Proverbs 3:5-6
Trust in the Lord with all your heart and lean not on your own understanding; in all your ways acknowledge him and he will make your paths straight.

Psalm 33:20-22
We wait in hope for the Lord; he is our help and our shield. In him our hearts rejoice, for we trust in his holy name. May your unfailing love be with us, Lord, even as we put our hope in you.

Job 23:10
But he knows the way that I take; when he has tested me, I will come forth as gold.

*I am still confident of this: I will see
the goodness of the Lord in the
land of the living.*

Psalm 27:13

Children proclaim the goodness of God with words of grace before a meal, "God is great, God is good…" But as we grow older and come face to face with tragedy or loss, doubts dim our certainty of it. Our view of His "goodness" comes to mean having a long, happy life, devoid of pain, suffering, failure, or loss. Yet God's ways are not our ways, nor His thoughts our thoughts. His goodness reveals itself most vividly when faith is being taken from the shallows to the deeper waters of waiting, hoping, and trusting in God alone for rescue or deliverance.

Confidence in God's goodness is based on the truth of the Scriptures and our past experience with His faithfulness. The writer of Psalm 27 has faced war, personal attack, and violence, yet the Psalmist has been confident… *The Lord is the stronghold of my life…*[v1] *My heart will not fear…*[v3] *In the day of trouble, he will keep me safe…*[v5] But when a new crisis arises, we may all be tempted to think God has hidden His face from us. All of a sudden confidence is wavering, and the Psalmist is calling out for mercy, seeking God's face, and begging Him not to forsake him or turn him over to his foes. Panic always blots out the memory of God's past goodness. But He hears our cries and responds with His heart-calming mercy and helpful provisions. Then once again we can be strong and confident because we have seen the goodness of the Lord in this life He has given us. Thanks be to God for His faithful goodness!

THANK GOD: Psalm 100:5 ▪ Psalm 119:68,71 ▪ Psalm 145:8-9
TRUST GOD: Isaiah 55:8 ▪ Nahum 1:7 ▪ James 1:2-3

Thank God:

Psalm 100:5
For the Lord is good and his love endures forever; his faithfulness continues through all generations.

Psalm 119:68, 71
You are good, and what you do is good; teach me your decrees.

It was good for me to be afflicted so that I might learn your decrees.

Psalm 145:8-9
The Lord is gracious and compassionate, slow to anger and rich in love. The Lord is good to all; he has compassion on all he has made.

Trust God:

Isaiah 55:8
"For my thoughts are not your thoughts, neither are your ways my ways," declares the Lord.

Nahum 1:7
The Lord is good, a refuge in times of trouble. He cares for those who trust in him...

James 1:2-3
Consider it pure joy, my brothers and sisters, whenever you face trials of many kinds, because you know that the testing of your faith produces perseverance.

Because of the Lord's great love, we are not consumed, for his compassions never fail. They are new every morning; great is your faithfulness.

Lamentations 3:22-23

How easily we forget God's goodness to us! We may have come through "many dangers, toils and snares," as John Newton wrote in "Amazing Grace," but in a new crisis, our confidence in God's caring falters in panic and doubt. Our human heart always reacts with some lament....so go to Lamentations and read words that promise the Lord's mercies are new <u>every</u> morning. Be encouraged that *the Lord is good to those whose hope is in him.* He shows compassion with his unfailing love.

If you know the song, "Great Is Thy Faithfulness," sing over and over the lines, "Morning by morning, new mercies I see" and "All I have needed his hand has provided; great is his faithfulness..." The Lord has given our hearts a deep capacity for faith when melody and words of truth are combined, sung not only with the lips, but with the heart. Hans Christian Anderson wisely spoke, "When words fail, music speaks."

My husband's worst business nightmare became my reality one summer after his death. Torrential, unrelenting rains collapsed a roof on our 100-year-old downtown commercial building. The potential financial consequences were mind-boggling and paralyzing....until I heard some singers, like angelic voices, singing, "Be still my soul...leave to thy God to order and provide..." The heart-stirring words became my song, my self-talk, my prayer. The long road to successful, up-to-code restoration was paved daily with new mercies from the God of unfailing love and compassion. May it be so in your next personal crisis.

THANK GOD: Psalm 46:1 ▪ Psalm 40:3 ▪ Lamentations 3:20-21,25
TRUST GOD: Psalm 107:5-6 ▪ Psalm 143:8 ▪ James 5:11

Thank God:

Psalm 46:1
God is our refuge and strength, an ever-present help in trouble.

Psalm 40:3
He put a new song in my mouth, a hymn of praise to our God. Many will see and fear the Lord and put their trust in him.

Lamentations 3:20-21, 25
I well remember them, and my soul is downcast within me. Yet this I call to mind and therefore I have hope...

The Lord is good to those whose hope is in him, to the one who seeks him...

Trust God:

Psalm 107:5-6
They were hungry and thirsty, and their lives ebbed away. Then they cried out to the Lord in their trouble, and he delivered them from their distress.

Psalm 143:8
Let the morning bring me word of your unfailing love, for I have put my trust in you. Show me the way I should go, for to you I entrust my life.

James 5:11
As you know, we count as blessed those who have persevered. You have heard of Job's perseverance and have seen what the Lord finally brought about. The Lord is full of compassion and mercy.

*The grass withers, the flowers fall, but
the word of our God stands forever.*

Isaiah 40:8

In this imperfect, fallen world, there is little that we can forever depend
on, except that change is going to be part of our lives. Changing ages
result in other changes....different sizes, tastes, choices, priorities,
friends, activities, abilities, and dreams. Yet, God, in His book, the Bible,
tells us that *Jesus Christ is the same yesterday and today and forever.*
(Hebrews 13:8) What a relief to know that God, the Father, and His Son,
our Savior, are not constantly evolving, or changing, or forgetting what
has been revealed in written form....God's word stands forever!

As we draw closer to the Lord by reading His word, some principles about His Lordship invite us to trust Him and His word more
completely:

> In regards to His promises....Yea and Amen.
> In regards to His timing....perfect....(but often it seems slow!).
> In regards to His perspective on timing....wait patiently.
> In regards to His answering prayer....yes, no, or wait.
> In regards to His perspective on obedience....now/today.

We cannot see or know all that our heavenly Father sees, knows,
and purposes for our lives. We can trust and obey what we do know,
continuing to learn more of His unchanging character and attributes.
Colossians 3:16 encourages believers to *let the word of Christ dwell in
you richly as you teach and admonish one another with all wisdom...* The
Bible is our source for those words of wisdom and life that stand forever
from an almighty and unchanging Sovereign God.

THANK GOD: Psalm 18:30 ▪ Psalm 31:14-15 ▪ II Corinthians 1:20
TRUST GOD: Deuteronomy 13:4 ▪ Psalm 27:13-14 ▪ Jeremiah 33:3

Thank God:

Psalm 18:30
As for God, his way is perfect: The Lord's word is flawless; he shields all who take refuge in him.

Psalm 31:14-15
But I trust in you, Lord; I say, "You are my God." My times are in your hands; deliver me from the hands of my enemies, from those who pursue me.

II Corinthians 1:20
For no matter how many promises God has made, they are "Yes" in Christ. And so through him the "Amen" is spoken by us to the glory of God.

Trust God:

Deuteronomy 13:4
It is the Lord your God you must follow, and him you must revere. Keep his commands and obey him; serve him and hold fast to him.

Psalm 27:13-14
I remain confident of this: I will see the goodness of the Lord in the land of the living. Wait for the Lord; be strong and take heart and wait for the Lord.

Jeremiah 33:3
Call to me and I will answer you and tell you great and unsearchable things you do not know.

Stand at the crossroads and look....
Ask where the good way is and walk in it,
and you will find rest for your souls.

Jeremiah 6:16

In a Jerusalem under siege, the prophet Jeremiah urged the beleaguered Hebrew people to walk in the faith of their forefathers....the Patriarchs and Kings who had trusted in God's direction, provision, and deliverance. But they refused. As Jerusalem fell, the rest-deprived residents went into captivity in Babylon. A similar urgency to seek God's provision for rest was spoken by Corrie ten Boom, survivor of a Nazi death camp during World War II: "If you look at the world, you will be distressed. If you look within, you will be depressed. But if you look at Christ, you'll be at rest." Only the Prince of Peace can give rest in the midst of horrific circumstances....the tortures of war and captivity, weather devastations, the ravages of terminal disease or the terror of a viral pandemic. Jesus gives the invitation to *come to me, all you who are weary and burdened, and I will give you rest.* (Matthew 11:28)

Are you standing at a crossroads today with few options, lacking resources and direction? Needed rest, recovery, restoration, or healing depend on God alone. Thankfully, your dire moment has not taken God by surprise. Ask Him for His way out of the dilemma, pain, or loss. Ask for His next step to give your soul an escape from the temptation to lose hope. In faith, rest your soul in His tender keeping, seek His wisdom and listen for His voice on which way to take. *Commit thy way unto the Lord; trust also in him, and he shall bring it to pass.*

THANK GOD: Psalm 62:5-6 ▪ James 1:5 ▪ Matthew 11:29
TRUST GOD: Proverbs 3:5-6 ▪ Isaiah 30:20-21 ▪ Psalm 37:5 KJV, 23-24

Thank God:

Psalm 62:5-6
Yes, my soul, find rest in God; my hope comes from him. Truly he is my rock and my salvation; he is my fortress, I will not be shaken.

James 1:5
If any of you lacks wisdom, you should ask God, who gives generously to all without finding fault, and it will be given to you.

Matthew 11:29
Take my yoke upon you and learn from me, for I am gentle and humble in heart, and you will find rest for your souls.

Trust God:

Proverbs 3:5-6
Trust in the Lord with all your heart and lean not on your own understanding; in all your ways acknowledge him and he will make your paths straight.

Isaiah 30:20-21
Although the Lord gives you the bread of adversity and the water of affliction, your teachers will be hidden no more; with your own eyes you will see them. Whether you turn to the right or to the left, your ears will hear a voice behind you, saying, "This is the way; walk in it."

Psalm 37:5 KJV, 23-24
Commit thy way unto the Lord; trust also in him; and he shall bring it to pass.

The Lord makes firm the steps of the one who delights in him; though he may stumble, he will not fall, for the Lord upholds him with his hand.

….those who receive God's
abundant provision of grace
and of the gift of righteousness reign in life
through the one man, Jesus Christ.

Romans 5: 17

To "reign in life" sounds like the ultimate aspiration. Few would turn down an opportunity to live above life's sin and death destiny which came into the world through the disobedience of Adam. But God offers us a means of grace by the death and resurrection of His Son, whereby we can be declared righteous to live "the life that is truly life"….not as the captain of our own fate, or the master of our own soul….but as His forgiven and redeemed son or daughter, enjoying abundant life now and eternal life after death. The universal truth that one man can make a difference was never more clearly illustrated. Through Adam, all were condemned to sin and death, but though Christ Jesus, all believers can reign in life, both now and in eternity.

    If reigning in life sounds impossible given your current crisis, health situation, or the overall brokenness of everything or everyone around you, take heart and hold tight to God's promises from Romans: *We know that in all things God works for the good of those who love Him, who have been called according to his purpose. If God is for us, who can be against us?….In all these things we are more than conquerors through Him who loved us.* Follow Abraham's example of faith: *Against all hope, he in hope believed* that, though childless, he would become a father of nations. *He did not waiver through unbelief…but was strengthened in his faith and gave God glory, being fully persuaded God had power to do what He had promised.* Claim God's promise! Reign in life through One!

THANK GOD: John 10:10 ▪ Romans 8:28, 31, 37 ▪ I Timothy 6:19
TRUST GOD: Romans 4:18, 21-22 ▪ Romans 5:12 ▪ II Timothy 2:1, 11-12

Thank God:

John 10:10
The thief comes only to steal and kill and destroy; I have come that they may have life, and have it to the full.

Romans 8:28, 31, 37
And we know that in all things God works for the good of those who love him, who have been called according to his purpose.

What, then, shall we say in response to these things? If God is for us, who can be against us?

In all these things we are more than conquerors through him who loved us.

I Timothy 6:19
In this way they will lay up treasure for themselves as a firm foundation for the coming age, so that they may take hold of the life that is truly life.

Trust God:

Romans 4:18, 21-22
Against all hope, Abraham in hope believed and so became the father of many nations....he did not waver through unbelief regarding the promise of God, but was strengthened in his faith and gave glory to God, being fully persuaded that God had power to do what he had promised.

Romans 5:12
Therefore, just as sin entered the world through one man, and death through sin, and in this way death came to all people, because all sinned...

II Timothy 2:1, 11-12
You then, my son, be strong in the grace that is in Jesus Christ.

Here is a trustworthy saying: If we died with him, we will also live with him; if we endure, we will also reign with him...

But as for me, I watch in hope for the Lord,
I wait for my God, my Savior;
my God will hear me.

Micah 7:7

"Watch and wait" was Micah's message to Israel as God forecast coming disastrous judgments on the divided nation. Watching in hope means mind-shifting from fear and panic to inviting the God of hope into our scary situation. His judgments are always right and just. God had already told Israel how to be His godly people. But not only were they idolatrous, they despised justice and distorted what was right, resulting in mistreatment of the poor and needy.

Yet God tempered His words of judgment with a note of comfort, a most important Bible prophesy: that out of tiny Bethlehem one day would come a ruler, a shepherd King, who would rule in the majesty of the name of the Lord….so all could live securely. When called to "watch and wait" for future events, it is tempting to try to DO something about every distressing situation. But as A.B. Simpson said, "God does not so much want us to do things as to let people see what He can do." Let us maintain integrity and honest service to God and others as we await the Lord's short-term and long-range plans.

Today you may be facing very scary news, or a heart-breaking decision, or an unwanted verdict from an unjust judge. All seem like punishing judgments. Release frustrations and fears to the God who knows, hears, and cares. Let Bible truths recast your vision of God's sovereignty. Our Lord promises His presence, so we are never alone, never forsaken, even in exile. We may be fearful of what is happening to us or around us, but God gives us hope in watching and waiting for Him. Jesus fulfilled Micah's prophesy, born to rescue, deliver, and rule.

THANK GOD: Deuteronomy 31:6 ▪ Psalm 27:1 ▪ Micah 5:2,4
TRUST GOD: Psalm 33:20-22 ▪ Psalm 130:5 ▪ Micah 6:8; 7:8-9

Thank God:

Deuteronomy 31:6
Be strong and courageous. Do not be afraid or terrified because of them, for the Lord your God goes with you; he will never leave you nor forsake you.

Psalm 27:1
The Lord is my light and my salvation—whom shall I fear? The Lord is the stronghold of my life—of whom shall I be afraid?

Micah 5:2, 4
But you, Bethlehem Ephrathah, though you are small among the clans of Judah, out of you will come for me one who will be ruler over Israel, whose origins are from of old, from ancient times.

He will stand and shepherd his flock in the strength of the Lord, in the majesty of the name of the Lord his God. And they will live securely, for then his greatness will reach to the ends of the earth.

Trust God:

Psalm 33:20-22
We wait in hope for the Lord; he is our help and our shield. In him our hearts rejoice, for we trust in his holy name. May your unfailing love be with us, Lord, even as we put our hope in you.

Psalm 130:5
I wait for the Lord, my whole being waits, and in his word I put my hope.

Micah 6:8; 7:8-9
He has shown you, O mortal, what is good. And what does the Lord require of you? To act justly and to love mercy and to walk humbly with your God.

Do not gloat over me, my enemy! Though I have fallen, I will rise. Though I sit in darkness, the Lord will be my light. Because I have sinned against him, I will bear the Lord's wrath, until he pleads my case and upholds my cause. He will bring me out into the light; I will see his righteousness.

We are hard pressed on every side,
but not crushed; perplexed, but not in
despair; persecuted, but not abandoned;
struck down, but not destroyed.

II Corinthians 4:8-9

Do any of those words describe you? Pressed? Perplexed? Persecuted? Struck down? How vivid are these expressions from the Apostle Paul whose unimaginably chaotic troubles could consume every ounce of mental and physical energy....imprisoned, flogged, stoned, shipwrecked, endangered by weather, hunger, thirst, and sleeplessness. Any one of those experiences can become a source of hopelessness. Yet each description of his condition is qualified by the word "but," counter-acting the negative reality and giving hope. When complaining negativity about a trying situation overtakes me, Lord, please change my perspective with reassuring words of hope from your Word.

Hard pressed, but not crushed....because God is the strength and the joy of my heart, and He will keep me in His peace when I am trusting Him. *Perplexed, but not in despair*....because God urges me to ask Him for wisdom in the face of a confusion-clouded mind or perhaps an indecision-induced paralysis. *Persecuted, but not abandoned*....because God has promised He will never leave me or forsake me, and Jesus declared, "I am with you always..." *Struck down, but not destroyed*....because God is a stronghold in the day of trouble, and He knows those who are trusting in Him (better than we know ourselves).

Whether God chooses to remove us from a dire situation or to hold our hand in an overcoming process, counter every hope-dasher by this affirmation: God is able to do more than we can ask, think, or imagine.

THANK GOD: Isaiah 26:3 ▪ Nahum 1:7 ▪ Ephesians 3:20
TRUST GOD: Matthew 28:20 ▪ Hebrews 13:5 ▪ James1:5

Thank God:

Isaiah 26:3
You will keep in perfect peace those whose minds are steadfast, because they trust in you.

Nahum 1:7
The Lord is good, a refuge in times of trouble. He cares for those who trust in him...

Ephesians 3:20
Now to him who is able to do immeasurably more than all we ask or imagine, according to his power that is at work within us...

Trust God:

Matthew 28:20
...and teaching them to obey everything I have commanded you. And surely I am with you always, to the very end of the age.

Hebrews 13:5
Keep your lives free from the love of money and be content with what you have, because God has said, "Never will I leave you; never will I forsake you."

James 1:5
If any of you lacks wisdom, you should ask God, who gives generously to all without finding fault, and it will be given to you.

You are my refuge and my shield. I have put my hope in your word.

Psalm 119: 114

To hope in God's word means I have to know where God's word is found and what it says about Him and His creations. Many loud and contradicting voices vie for my attention, but God's voice speaks gently to me when, with listening ears, I read the Bible as His words to me. Yet before God's words can transform my mind and heart, I must believe by faith that He exists, and He is a rewarder of those who earnestly seek Him. The Psalmist knows God is a refuge and shield, because he has experienced it. *He is a shield for all who take refuge in Him.* What hope-filled words! Our God is a shield from fiery darts of an enemy and a place of refuge and protection for His embattled people.

John Newton, the writer of "Amazing Grace," undoubtedly knew Psalm 119 with its multiple verses about putting hope in God's word. The third verse of his hymn proclaims, "The Lord has promised good to me / His word my hope secures / He will my shield and portion be / as long as life endures." When next you hear the strains of this song of faith, rejoice that the Lord has not left us to guess about His words and promises. He has recorded them in the Bible for all to read and to believe that He is the eternal, Almighty God whose Word stands forever. But God's hope-filled word to mankind is not just His written word. He has sent His Son, Jesus, as the living Word. *The Word was made flesh and dwelt among us.* He was sent in love to speak for His Father, to redeem us from sin, and make it possible for us to live forever with Him.

THANK GOD: Genesis 15:1 ▪ Psalm 18:30 ▪ John 1:14
TRUST GOD: Psalm 119:81 ▪ Isaiah 40:8 ▪ Hebrews 11:5

Thank God:

Genesis 15:1
After this, the word of the Lord came to Abram in a vision: "Do not be afraid, Abram. I am your shield, your very great reward."

Psalm 18:30
As for God, his way is perfect: The Lord's word is flawless; he shields all who take refuge in him.

John 1:14
The Word became flesh and made his dwelling among us. We have seen his glory, the glory of the one and only Son, who came from the Father, full of grace and truth.

Trust God:

Psalm 119:81
My soul faints with longing for your salvation, but I have put my hope in your word.

Isaiah 40:8
The grass withers and the flowers fall, but the word of our God endures forever.

Hebrews 11:5
By faith Enoch was taken from this life, so that he did not experience death: "He could not be found, because God had taken him away." For before he was taken, he was commended as one who pleased God.

Let us not become weary in doing good; for at the proper time we will reap a harvest if we do not give up.

Galatians 6:9

Have you ever felt frustrated by a sense of helplessness if year after year you have sought to nudge a friend closer to the Lord? You share your thankfulness for many blessings God has given, including their friendship. You repeatedly invite this person to church or Bible study, or try to find one-on-one chat time at a gathering. You are weary in well-doing, even though you felt the Lord calling you to show this person special kindness in His name. Galatians 6:9 is an encouragement not to give up, to keep on keeping on, until the "proper time"....which God alone determines. Take heart! Be encouraged as you persevere!

The prophet Jeremiah may be God's best example of not giving up. His call was to persuade the Southern Kingdom of Judah to repent from idolatry, to forsake their worship of many gods and love the one true God. His pronouncements of impending judgment and destruction fell on deaf ears year after year. God's people ignored the warnings. The king sought to silence Jeremiah, putting him in prison. Doomsday came, and most of God's people were carried into exile by the Babylonians. Jerusalem was destroyed. But God's judgment was not His final word. Jeremiah's message to the exiles became one of hope: God still had plans to prosper them again in the land promised to His people long ago.

Are you thinking of giving up on something or someone God has pressed upon your heart? Persevere in hope, trusting God's mighty hand and perfect timing to accomplish His purposes through you.

THANK GOD: Jeremiah 32:17, 26-27 ▪ II Corinthians 9:8 ▪ Galatians 6:10
TRUST GOD: Proverbs 3:5-6 ▪ Jeremiah 33:6 ▪ Jeremiah 29:11-13

Thank God:

Jeremiah 32:17, 26-27
Ah, Sovereign Lord, you have made the heavens and the earth by your great power and outstretched arm. Nothing is too hard for you.

Then the word of the Lord came to Jeremiah: "I am the Lord, the God of all mankind. Is anything too hard for me?"

II Corinthians 9:8
And God is able to bless you abundantly, so that in all things at all times, having all that you need, you will abound in every good work.

Galatians 6:10
Therefore, as we have opportunity, let us do good to all people, especially to those who belong to the family of believers.

Trust God:

Proverbs 3:5-6
Trust in the Lord with all your heart and lean not on your own understanding; in all your ways acknowledge him and he will make your paths straight.

Jeremiah 33:6
Nevertheless, I will bring health and healing to it; I will heal my people and will let them enjoy abundant peace and security.

Jeremiah 29:11-13
"For I know the plans I have for you," declares the Lord, "plans to prosper you and not to harm you, plans to give you hope and a future. Then you will call on me and come and pray to me, and I will listen to you. You will seek me and find me when you seek me with all your heart."

....Be careful, keep calm and do not be afraid.
Do not lose heart.....

Isaiah 7:4

God has a way of giving simple but powerful advice to sustain us during times of prolonged stress. These four commands, given by God to Isaiah for a Judean king, advised him regarding his fears in the face of overwhelming enemies. During the stressful years of my late husband's illness, I prayed each phrase daily, believing that God was still using His words in Scripture to give counsel, comfort, and hope to fearful hearts:

Lord, may I "be careful," watchful, cautious, and vigilant whether listening to medical information and instructions or carrying them out. Let me choose my words carefully to be an encouragement to bravery.

May I "keep calm," not given to panic. So focus my mind on You that your peace is conveyed to my patient even when painful, scary, and repetitive treatments must be administered. Remind me of your abiding presence. Please, let a calm confidence prevail in my voice and words.

Oh, Lord, fear is beginning to fill my heart and mind amidst the fog of decision-making, unpredictable outcomes, and an uncertain future. You always say, "Do not be afraid," and experience has taught me You have the power and will to make that a reality. So today I cast my fears, cares, and anxieties on You, trusting in your unfailing love and mercy.

Heavenly Father, your word challenges me: "Do not lose heart," but rather, take heart and be encouraged. I hold on to hope in Jesus who says to me: *In this world you will have trouble. But take heart, I have overcome the world.* Jesus has won the victory for us, even over death. Amen!

THANK GOD: Isaiah 26:3 ▪ Isaiah 41:10 ▪ John 16:33
TRUST GOD: Psalm 33:20-22 ▪ Psalm 56:3-4 ▪ Romans 5:5, 15:13

Thank God:

Isaiah 26:3
You will keep in perfect peace those whose minds are steadfast, because they trust in you.

Isaiah 41:10
So do not fear, for I am with you; do not be dismayed, for I am your God. I will strengthen you and help you; I will uphold you with my righteous right hand.

John 16:33
I have told you these things, so that in me you may have peace. In this world you will have trouble. But take heart! I have overcome the world.

Trust God:

Psalm 33:20-22
We wait in hope for the Lord; he is our help and our shield. In him our hearts rejoice, for we trust in his holy name. May your unfailing love be with us, Lord, even as we put our hope in you.

Psalm 56:3-4
When I am afraid, I put my trust in you. In God, whose word I praise—in God I trust and am not afraid. What can mere mortals do to me?

Romans 5:5, 15:13
And hope does not put us to shame, because God's love has been poured out into our hearts through the Holy Spirit, who has been given to us.

May the God of hope fill you with all joy and peace as you trust in him, so that you may overflow with hope by the power of the Holy Spirit.

*My grace is sufficient for you, for my power
is made perfect in weakness.*

II Corinthians 12:9

A prime example of how God's thoughts and ways are higher than ours is the concept of weakness being the place where God perfects His power and strength. This puzzling principle means weakness can be a positive, instead of a negative! Weakness may be the result of fatigue, weariness, illness, injury, grief, or even just lack of exercise. But when it is self-acknowledged, prompting a true dependency on our powerful but gracious God, then His grace supplies the strength that overcomes our weakness. Our trust matures with each moment His sufficient grace strengthens our bodies, our minds, our hearts, and our wills to do His will.

Persistent weakness robs us of hope, no matter the origin or how valiantly or sacrificially we have expended our self-efforts. An enemy is always seeking to exploit our weaknesses with targeted attacks. But God encourages us to commit our way to Him. *For the battle is not yours, but God's.* When we by faith entrust our weakness to Him, we become aware of the exchange as a platform for the display of His power and goodness. Seeing the Lord engineer our comeback from weakness or defeat glorifies Him and renews hope for others.

Dependency is not a popular trait among subscribers to the self-sufficient, self-sovereign model of life. But those deeply dependent on the Lord for anything and everything have a humility that gives them even more grace. They will join the chorus of those who are singing these words, *For when I am weak, then I am strong.* Thanks be to God!

THANK GOD: II Chronicles 20:15 ▪ Isaiah 40:29-31 ▪ II Corinthians 12:10
TRUST GOD: Isaiah 55:8-9 ▪ James 4:6 ▪ Hebrews 4:16

Thank God:

II Chronicles 20:15

He said: "Listen, King Jehoshaphat and all who live in Judah and Jerusalem! This is what the Lord says to you: 'Do not be afraid or discouraged because of this vast army. For the battle is not yours, but God's.'"

Isaiah 40:29-31

He gives strength to the weary and increases the power of the weak. Even youths grow tired and weary, and young men stumble and fall; but those who hope in the Lord will renew their strength. They will soar on wings like eagles; they will run and not grow weary, they will walk and not be faint.

II Corinthians 12:10

That is why, for Christ's sake, I delight in weaknesses, in insults, in hardships, in persecutions, in difficulties. For when I am weak, then I am strong.

Trust God:

Isaiah 55:8-9

"For my thoughts are not your thoughts, neither are your ways my ways," declares the Lord. "As the heavens are higher than the earth, so are my ways higher than your ways and my thoughts than your thoughts."

James 4:6

But he gives us more grace. That is why Scripture says: "God opposes the proud but shows favor to the humble."

Hebrews 4:16

Let us then approach God's throne of grace with confidence, so that we may receive mercy and find grace to help us in our time of need.

In the morning, O Lord, you hear my voice;
in the morning I lay my requests before you
and wait in expectation.

Psalm 5:3

Friends often classify themselves as either "a morning person" or "a night owl." Of course, God made them both, but the morning folks have a head start on their day with God. Multiple Scriptures refer to God's activity at an early hour, and many of His servants seek Him then. Abraham, Joshua, Gideon, Samuel, and David all communed with God early in the day. Moses' words might well be our own prayer to God every day: *Satisfy us in the morning with your unfailing love, that we may sing for joy and be glad all our days.* (Psalm 90:14)

One caution God gives is not to bless your neighbor in a loud voice early in the morning, as it will be taken as a curse! (Proverbs 27:14) With care and humor, God watches out for the sleepy-head night owls, too.

God's compassions never fail; they are new every morning. The prophet Isaiah asked God to be gracious to His people, to be their strength every morning, especially in stressful times. Morning offers a quiet time before daily distractions or struggles of the workplace compete for our attention and focus. Solitude enables our hearts to hear God's words of encouragement or exhortation. Jesus Himself rose up early in the morning, while it was still dark, to pray in preparation for preaching and teaching. When you go to bed with concerns and anxieties, pour out your heart to the Lord by praying these words from God's Word as you go to sleep: *Let the morning bring me word of your unfailing love, for I have put my trust in you.* (Psalm 143:8)

THANK GOD: Psalm 30:5 ▪ Lamentations 3:22-23 ▪ Mark 1:35
TRUST GOD: Psalm 88:13 ▪ Psalm 119:147 ▪ Isaiah 33:2

Thank God:

Psalm 30:5
For his anger lasts only a moment, but his favor lasts a lifetime; weeping may stay for the night, but rejoicing comes in the morning.

Lamentations 3:22-23
Because of the Lord's great love we are not consumed, for his compassions never fail. They are new every morning; great is your faithfulness.

Mark 1:35
Very early in the morning, while it was still dark, Jesus got up, left the house and went off to a solitary place, where he prayed.

Trust God:

Psalm 88:13
But I cry to you for help, Lord; in the morning my prayer comes before you.

Psalm 119:147
I rise before dawn and cry for help; I have put my hope in your word.

Isaiah 33:2
Lord, be gracious to us; we long for you. Be our strength every morning, our salvation in time of distress.

We live by faith and not by sight.

II Corinthians 5:7

Without faith it is impossible to please God, because anyone who comes to him must believe that he exists and that he rewards those who earnestly seek him. (Hebrews 11:5) Whether we have little faith, much faith, or great faith, God knows, and He wants us to seek Him. With even a sliver of faith, draw near to Him in hope because He is there, and He cares. Jesus encouraged His followers with a small-step approach, saying that faith as small as a mustard seed (which looks like a speck of ground black pepper) has the potential to grow into a huge bush. A tiny but growing faith in Him can be powerful enough to move mountains.

Today, "having faith" can pertain to market forces, the value of gold or silver, weather patterns, or a leader's charisma or self-confidence. But in Scripture, the object of our faith is the key to becoming a mountain mover. *Trust in the Lord with all your heart... Have faith in the Lord your God, and you will be upheld. It is Jesus' name and the faith that comes through him* that accomplishes miracles. Is the Lord Jesus Christ the object of your faith, or is something else?

The disciple Thomas expressed doubts about the resurrected Jesus....but he was graciously shown the nail marks on Jesus' hands. Thomas then exclaimed, "My Lord and My God!" But Jesus in prayer to His heavenly Father commends those who believe in Him by faith alone and not by sight only. Thankfully, that includes you and me. *Blessed are those who have not seen and yet have believed.*

THANK GOD: II Chronicles 20:20 ▪ Proverbs 3:5-6 ▪ Acts 3:16
TRUST GOD: Psalm 22:4-5 ▪ Matthew 17:20 ▪ John 20:24-29

Thank God:

II Chronicles 20:20

Early in the morning they left for the Desert of Tekoa. As they set out, Jehoshaphat stood and said, "Listen to me, Judah and people of Jerusalem! Have faith in the Lord your God and you will be upheld; have faith in his prophets and you will be successful."

Proverbs 3:5-6

Trust in the Lord with all your heart and lean not on your own understanding; in all your ways acknowledge him and he will make your paths straight.

Acts 3:16

By faith in the name of Jesus, this man whom you see and know was made strong. It is Jesus' name and the faith that comes through him that has completely healed him, as you can all see.

Trust God:

Psalm 22:4-5

In you our ancestors put their trust; they trusted and you delivered them. To you they cried out and were saved; in you they trusted and were not put to shame.

John 20:24-29

Now Thomas (also known as Didymus), one of the Twelve, was not with the disciples when Jesus came. So the other disciples told him, "We have seen the Lord!" But he said to them, "Unless I see the nail marks in his hands and put my finger where the nails were, and put my hand into his side, I will not believe." A week later his disciples were in the house again, and Thomas was with them. Though the doors were locked, Jesus came and stood among them and said, "Peace be with you!" Then he said to Thomas, "Put your finger here; see my hands. Reach out your hand and put it into my side. Stop doubting and believe." Thomas said to him, "My Lord and my God!" Then Jesus told him, "Because you have seen me, you have believed; blessed are those who have not seen and yet have believed."

What is man that you are mindful of him,
the son of man that you care for him?

Psalm 8:4 Psalm 144:3 Hebrews 2:6

When you survey the starry heavens, gaze at endless mountain peaks, or witness the powerful crashing of a magnificent waterfall, do you ever have that "speck of dust" feeling about yourself? You are not alone....in at least three places in the Bible, the writers raise the same question of God. His creation alone dwarfs our self-importance, yet it is designed to draw us closer to the Creator. He knows how we are formed, remembers we are dust (Psalm 103:14), but does not leave us in a heap. Throughout God's Word, we are assured of His thoughts and care. Beloved by the One whose name is majestic in all the earth, we were "made a little lower than the angels" and crowned with glory and honor. No other living creature is blessed with those distinctions. Made in His image, mankind is at the center of God's heart....so do not despair or give way to resignation when overwhelmed by the vastness of the universe.

Let humble gratitude eclipse a fatalistic inferiority. When next you are awed by the wonders of earth, sea, and sky, turn to Colossians 1 where Jesus is revealed as the Father's co-Creator....for by Him and for Him were all things made, and in Him all things are held together. So instead of dismay, rejoice and give thanks for creation's miraculous design, letting it draw you close to *the God of hope* who *will fill you with joy and peace in believing.* His promise is never to leave you or forsake you. His thoughts and cares will lift you from smallness to security as a beloved of the Creator, who thinks and cares about you.

THANK GOD: Psalm 8:1,3,5 ▪ Romans 15:13 ▪ Colossians 1:15-17
TRUST GOD: Deuteronomy 31:6, 33:2 ▪ Hebrews 13:6 ▪ I Peter 5:6-7

Thank God:

Psalm 8:1, 3, 5
Lord, our Lord, how majestic is your name in all the earth! You have set your glory in the heavens.

When I consider your heavens, the work of your fingers, the moon and the stars, which you have set in place...

You have made [mankind] a little lower than the angels and crowned them with glory and honor.

Romans 15:13
May the God of hope fill you with all joy and peace as you trust in him, so that you may overflow with hope by the power of the Holy Spirit.

Colossians 1:15-17
The Son is the image of the invisible God, the firstborn over all creation. For in him all things were created: things in heaven and on earth, visible and invisible, whether thrones or powers or rulers or authorities; all things have been created through him and for him. He is before all things, and in him all things hold together.

Trust God:

Deuteronomy 31:6, 33:2
Be strong and courageous. Do not be afraid or terrified because of them, for the Lord your God goes with you; he will never leave you nor forsake you.

He said: "The Lord came from Sinai and dawned over them from Seir; he shone forth from Mount Paran. He came with myriads of holy ones from the south, from his mountain slopes."

Hebrews 13:6
So we say with confidence, "The Lord is my helper; I will not be afraid. What can mere mortals do to me?"

I Peter 5:6-7
Humble yourselves, therefore, under God's mighty hand, that he may lift you up in due time. Cast all your anxiety on him because he cares for you.

*Always be prepared to give an answer to
everyone who asks you to give the reason for
the hope you have.*

I Peter 3:15

When God has given new hope to your heart, before long someone will notice a change in your countenance. They may ask you about the difference. No need to panic! It is the next step in being blessed to be a blessing. Just state simply, with a smile, that you have trusted God for His words of truth and claimed them for yourself. How the Spirit accomplishes the hope renewal you might not be able to explain precisely. But just as we cannot record the exact moment when night becomes day, we do know for sure when darkness has become light.

If you have taken to heart God's words about a living hope in Jesus, welcome a question about your hope. To be more ready, remember conversational techniques suggested in the Scripture. Peter's caution is *to do this with gentleness and respect.* Colossians 3:5-6 is a model.... *Be wise in the way you act toward outsiders; make the most of every opportunity. Let your conversation be always full of grace, seasoned with salt, so that you may know how to answer everyone.* With a grateful heart, acknowledge God's grace in the process of hope renewal. Invite an inquirer to ask God for their own need, be it for salvation, hope, strength, courage, or maybe their next meal or house payment. Share a Bible verse the Lord has given you to hold on to. God is faithful to all who call upon Him in truth. So be prepared and ready, be gentle and inviting....be a blessing that opens a window of hope for another heart!

THANK GOD: Psalm 145:17-18 ▪ Romans 10:12 ▪ I Peter 1:3
TRUST GOD: Psalm 73:28 ▪ II Corinthians 4:4-6 ▪ I Peter 2:9

Thank God:

Psalm 145:17-18
The Lord is righteous in all his ways and faithful in all he does. The Lord is near to all who call on him, to all who call on him in truth.

Romans 10:12
For there is no difference between Jew and Gentile—the same Lord is Lord of all and richly blesses all who call on him...

I Peter 1:3
Praise be to the God and Father of our Lord Jesus Christ! In his great mercy he has given us new birth into a living hope through the resurrection of Jesus Christ from the dead...

Trust God:

Psalm 73:28
But as for me, it is good to be near God. I have made the Sovereign Lord my refuge; I will tell of all your deeds.

II Corinthians 4:4-6
The god of this age has blinded the minds of unbelievers, so that they cannot see the light of the gospel that displays the glory of Christ, who is the image of God. For what we preach is not ourselves, but Jesus Christ as Lord, and ourselves as your servants for Jesus' sake. For God, who said, "Let light shine out of darkness," made his light shine in our hearts to give us the light of the knowledge of God's glory displayed in the face of Christ.

I Peter 2:9
But you are a chosen people, a royal priesthood, a holy nation, God's special possession, that you may declare the praises of him who called you out of darkness into his wonderful light.

Taste and see the Lord is good; blessed is the man who takes refuge in him.

Psalm 34:8

The days of both working women and stay-at-home mothers are filled with demands from sunrise to sunset, leaving little time for developing a relationship with God through Bible study. Arrow prayers each day or prayers at bedtime are about as much spiritual life as many can handle. And so it was that my godly mother began to hostess a once-a-month friendship luncheon group at her home called "Tasters". The purpose was to "taste and see the Lord is good" and to grow in our knowledge and love of Him together. A time of fellowship and delicious fare provided the backdrop for learning that the Scriptures are God's words for living in His presence and power, regardless of age, stage, or season of life. The Lord prospered "Tasters" for many years.

Monthly, we each chose a Bible verse to memorize; we then shared with each other about how God used that verse to impact us. We began to "taste and see" God's goodness, and we learned to trust Him more by hearing ways He had also worked on behalf of others. As we sought to know the Lord Himself by trusting His word, the result, as promised, was blessing! Whether you knew God for yourself before you came, or had never opened a Bible or believed God for His word, the shared laughter and tears, joys, and sorrows were encouragement and hope for each heart. Long after the "Tasters" years ended, we still recall them with joyful and thankful remembrance. Together we had, indeed, tasted and seen God's goodness and blessings for ourselves and others.

THANK GOD: Psalm 100:5 ▪ Psalm 31:19 ▪ Psalm 52:9
TRUST GOD: Psalm 27:13 ▪ Philippians 1:6 ▪ I Peter 2:2-3

Thank God:

Psalm 100:5
For the Lord is good and his love endures forever; his faithfulness continues through all generations.

Psalm 31:19
How abundant are the good things that you have stored up for those who fear you, that you bestow in the sight of all, on those who take refuge in you.

Psalm 52:9
For what you have done I will always praise you in the presence of your faithful people. And I will hope in your name, for your name is good.

Trust God:

Psalm 27:13
I remain confident of this: I will see the goodness of the Lord in the land of the living.

Philippians 1:6
I thank my God every time I remember you.

I Peter 2:2-3
Like newborn babies, crave pure spiritual milk, so that by it you may grow up in your salvation, now that you have tasted that the Lord is good.

*In the multitude of my thoughts within
me thy comforts delight my soul.*

Psalm 94:19 KJV

*When anxiety was great within me,
your consolation brought joy to my soul.*

Psalm 94:19 NIV

The multitude of thoughts and great anxiety within may have roots in a crisis of health, of heart, or of hope....a frightening medical diagnosis, a betrayal by a friend or family member, the loss of a life-long love, a future clouded by financial losses, or the threat of a lawsuit. Whatever the origin of the anxiety, your heavenly Father desires to calm your storm. As the "God of all comfort," our Lord is able to bring consolation to us in amazing ways. The dismayed and downcast soul, refocused on Him, can still experience delight and joy, increasing trust and renewing hope. Impossible? Improbable? Not for our Creator.

Recall any times past when God comforted your heart and soul? Is there a pattern that repeats itself? The God who made you knows the best way to remind you of His presence and care. He knows right where you are! You may hear a particular verse of Scripture several times in one day via media, Bible reading, or a friend's conversation. Listen closely to background music playing somewhere. Catch the tune of a spiritual song or hear lyrics that speak comfort to your heart. Family's voice on the phone or a timely sighting of a favorite woodpecker or cardinal are not coincidences. I call them God-winks or heavenly hugs. Learn to look and listen for His patterns of consolation in your life to bring joy and delight to your soul as you realize God is comforting <u>you</u>!

THANK GOD: Proverbs 12:25 ▪ Matthew 5:4 ▪ Psalm 119:49-50
TRUST GOD: Psalm 119:76-77 ▪ Philippians 4:6-7 ▪ I Peter 5:6-7

Thank God:

Proverbs 12:25
Anxiety weighs down the heart, but a kind word cheers it up.

Matthew 5:4
Blessed are those who mourn, for they will be comforted.

Psalm 119:49-50
Remember your word to your servant, for you have given me hope. My comfort in my suffering is this: Your promise preserves my life.

Trust God:

Psalm 119:76-77
May your unfailing love be my comfort, according to your promise to your servant. Let your compassion come to me that I may live, for your law is my delight.

Philippians 4:6-7
Do not be anxious about anything, but in every situation, by prayer and petition, with thanksgiving, present your requests to God. And the peace of God, which transcends all understanding, will guard your hearts and your minds in Christ Jesus.

I Peter 5:6-7
Humble yourselves, therefore, under God's mighty hand, that he may lift you up in due time. Cast all your anxiety on him because he cares for you.

I am the Lord, the God of all mankind.
Is anything too hard for me?

Jeremiah 32:27

Is anything too hard for God?

Genesis 18:14

God's rhetorical questions in the Bible teach us about His ways with mankind. Is anything too hard for God? He Himself first asked the question of Abraham, who doubted God's word about his wife, Sarah, bearing a son in old age. God asked the question again of Jeremiah as He prompted him to buy land on the eve of Israel's exile into faraway Babylonia. When the virgin Mary questioned the angel's news that she would have a Son conceived by the Holy Spirit, the angel replied, "Nothing is impossible with God."

God shows His power by doing what is impossible for us. He showed His love by sending His Son, Jesus, *who for the joy that was set before him endured the cross....*but is now resurrected from death and seated at the Father's right hand. Mankind has no power over death. All will die because all have sinned. But God has conquered sin and death through the sacrificial death of His Son. Jesus lives to give us life.

Is your heart troubled by past sins and failures, by someone else's poor choices, by heart-breaking losses beyond your control? Thank Jesus today for dying in your place to make the impossible possible: an abundant life now and eternal life with Him. Trust His power to fulfill every promise God has made in His word....even if it seems impossible. You can trust a man who has died for you! Jesus *is the resurrection and the life....*and nothing is too hard for the God of the Impossible!

THANK GOD: Jeremiah 32:17 ▪ John 11:25 ▪ Hebrews 12:2
TRUST GOD: Matthew 19:25-26 ▪ Romans 4:19-20, 5:12,8 ▪ Luke 1:37

Thank God:

Jeremiah 32:17
Ah, Sovereign Lord, you have made the heavens and the earth by your great power and outstretched arm. Nothing is too hard for you.

John 11:25
Jesus said to her, "I am the resurrection and the life. The one who believes in me will live, even though they die…"

Hebrews 12:2
…fixing our eyes on Jesus, the pioneer and perfecter of faith. For the joy set before him he endured the cross, scorning its shame, and sat down at the right hand of the throne of God.

Trust God:

Matthew 19:25-26
When the disciples heard this, they were greatly astonished and asked, "Who then can be saved?" Jesus looked at them and said, "With man this is impossible, but with God all things are possible."

Romans 4:19-20, 5:12, 8
Without weakening in his faith, he faced the fact that his body was as good as dead—since he was about a hundred years old—and that Sarah's womb was also dead. Yet he did not waver through unbelief regarding the promise of God, but was strengthened in his faith and gave glory to God…

…just as sin entered the world through one man, and death through sin, and in this way death came to all people, because all sinned…

But God demonstrates his own love for us in this: While we were still sinners, Christ died for us.

Luke 1:37
For no word from God will ever fail.

And my God shall meet all of your needs,
according to his glorious riches in Christ Jesus.

Philippians 4:19

Manna was God's provision of food for the Hebrews in the years of wilderness wandering after their miraculous exodus from Egypt. This bread-like substance was found each morning to be eaten that day. It spoiled if stored overnight, except on the day before the Sabbath, a day of worship and rest, when the gathering lasted for two days. For years God replenished the supply of manna in the same 6-day pattern.

Hope is a lot like that manna. Maintaining hope requires a daily gathering of truth from God's word. The manna analogy really applies to life when yesterday's hopes are dashed by disappointing, sudden, even irreversible changes in our situation. Loss of hope can lead to depression...it is always a challenge to our faith. Manna is needed.

If you are hungry for hope, turn to the gracious God of hope. He wants to give you joy and peace in believing and trusting Jesus, no matter how hopeless your feelings or situation. Open the Bible to Psalm 42. Identify with one whose tears have been his food day and night, who in despair recalls former times of festivity, thanksgiving, and joy. Pour out your needy, troubled heart to God in prayer. His promise is to be with you always and to meet your needs. Read His word until you hear His whisper of hope. Be like Abraham who against hope believed in hope, fully persuaded that what God had promised He was able to perform. Believe that God can meet your needs and renew your hope today as you seek to cope....and you, too, shall yet praise Him.

THANK GOD: Exodus 16:4 ▪ Deuteronomy 8:2-3 ▪ Psalm 16:8
TRUST GOD: Psalm 38:9-10 ▪ Psalm 42:5, 11 ▪ Romans 4:20-21, 15:13

Thank God:

Exodus 16:4
Then the Lord said to Moses, "I will rain down bread from heaven for you. The people are to go out each day and gather enough for that day. In this way I will test them and see whether they will follow my instructions."

Deuteronomy 8:2-3
Remember how the Lord your God led you all the way in the wilderness these forty years, to humble and test you in order to know what was in your heart, whether or not you would keep his commands. He humbled you, causing you to hunger and then feeding you with manna, which neither you nor your ancestors had known, to teach you that man does not live on bread alone but on every word that comes from the mouth of the Lord.

Psalm 16:8
I keep my eyes always on the Lord. With him at my right hand, I will not be shaken.

Trust God:

Psalm 38:9-10
All my longings lie open before you, Lord; my sighing is not hidden from you. My heart pounds, my strength fails me; even the light has gone from my eyes.

Psalm 42:5, 11
Why, my soul, are you downcast? Why so disturbed within me? Put your hope in God, for I will yet praise him, my Savior and my God.

Romans 4:20-21, 15:13
Yet he did not waver through unbelief regarding the promise of God, but was strengthened in his faith and gave glory to God, being fully persuaded that God had power to do what he had promised.

May the God of hope fill you with all joy and peace as you trust in him, so that you may overflow with hope by the power of the Holy Spirit.

*I wait for the Lord, my soul waits, and
in his word I put my hope.*

Psalm 130:5

The Psalmist is crying out to God, begging for Him to hear and be attentive to his cries for mercy. Reminders of human faults, mistakes, sins, and shortcomings prompt a question: Who can stand if God keeps a record of our sins? Needed forgiveness is addressed only by believing and affirming God's words about redemption. The writer is waiting in hope for that moment. In whom or what are you putting your hope for forgiveness and redemption? Is it in God's written word, recorded in Scripture and in the living word, God's Son, Jesus Christ? Or is it in your personal abilities or intellect, generous philanthropy, political power, or prestige? All of those can be gone in an instant. *But the word of our God stands forever.* In His abiding love, full redemption is His.

Skeptics scoff at the thought of believing words written by multiple authors, inspired by the Holy Spirit, recorded thousands of years ago. The Bible itself warns that detractors and deniers will laugh at those putting their hope in God's word.... at those who have come to know the Lord to be true to His word and sufficient for every need. God is so desirous of a relationship with us that He is open to a sincere "show me" attitude when the truth and power of His words are in question. The Lord is the God who knows all things, including the thoughts of our hearts. And He weighs motives....whether a scoffer's challenge is only an attitude of belligerence and defiance or a sincere hunger for the truth: God's words about His forgiveness and His redeeming grace.

THANK GOD: Isaiah 40:8 ▪ Colossians 1:13-14 ▪ Hebrews 4:12,16
TRUST GOD: II Chronicles 7:14 ▪ Psalm 130:1-4,7 ▪ Romans 3:23-24

Thank God:

Isaiah 40:8
The grass withers and the flowers fall, but the word of our God endures forever.

Colossians 1:13-14
For he has rescued us from the dominion of darkness and brought us into the kingdom of the Son he loves, in whom we have redemption, the forgiveness of sins.

Hebrews 4:12, 16
For the word of God is alive and active. Sharper than any double-edged sword, it penetrates even to dividing soul and spirit, joints and marrow; it judges the thoughts and attitudes of the heart.

Let us then approach God's throne of grace with confidence, so that we may receive mercy and find grace to help us in our time of need.

Trust God:

II Chronicles 7:14
...if my people, who are called by my name, will humble themselves and pray and seek my face and turn from their wicked ways, then I will hear from heaven, and I will forgive their sin and will heal their land.

Psalm 130:1-4, 7
Out of the depths I cry to you, Lord; Lord, hear my voice. Let your ears be attentive to my cry for mercy. If you, Lord, kept a record of sins, Lord, who could stand? But with you there is forgiveness, so that we can, with reverence, serve you.

Israel, put your hope in the Lord, for with the Lord is unfailing love and with him is full redemption.

Romans 3:23-24
...for all have sinned and fall short of the glory of God, and all are justified freely by his grace through the redemption that came by Christ Jesus.

*....We do not know what to do,
but our eyes are upon you.*

II Chronicles 20:12

What do you do when you do not know what to do?? At the end of our wit and wisdom, we must learn to humble ourselves under God's mighty hand and confess to Him our helplessness, as King Jehoshaphat did when facing overwhelming odds: "We do not know what to do, but our eyes are upon you." (Be thrilled as you read II Chronicles 20:1-30 to see what God did in response to a king's humble, honest prayer, and his people singing and praising God for the splendor of His holiness.)

Fixing our spiritual eyes, not our physical eyes, on our Sovereign God changes our focus from challenges, trials, or enemies to seeking His will and wisdom for times of crisis. "Commit your way to the Lord; trust in him and He will act." (Psalm 37:5 ESV) Commit a crisis by praying, trusting in His faithfulness. God instructs us to ask for wisdom when we need it. Sing and praise Him for the "splendor of his holiness" and for His enduring love. Rest on the promise that "the battle is not yours, but God's." Then, in faith, go without fear and face the enemy or challenge, confident that what God has promised, He is able to perform.

Whether you are a general, a farmer, a national leader, a student, business owner, teacher, doctor, soldier, pastor, homemaker, waitress, salesperson, lawyer, volunteer, banker, or busboy....no matter your position, profession, or place, next time you just "do not know what to do," remember II Chronicles 20. Look to the Lord, call upon Him in faith, then *stand firm and see the deliverance the Lord will give you.*

THANK GOD: II Chronicles 20:15, 17 ▪ Proverbs 11:2 ▪ James 1:5
TRUST GOD: Proverbs 3:5-6 ▪ Romans 4:21 ▪ I Peter 5:6-7

Thank God:

II Chronicles 20:15, 17
He said: "Listen, King Jehoshaphat and all who live in Judah and Jerusalem! This is what the Lord says to you: 'Do not be afraid or discouraged because of this vast army. For the battle is not yours, but God's...

'You will not have to fight this battle. Take up your positions; stand firm and see the deliverance the Lord will give you, Judah and Jerusalem. Do not be afraid; do not be discouraged. Go out to face them tomorrow, and the Lord will be with you.'"

Proverbs 11:2
When pride comes, then comes disgrace, but with humility comes wisdom.

James 1:5
If any of you lacks wisdom, you should ask God, who gives generously to all without finding fault, and it will be given to you.

Trust God:

Proverbs 3:5-6
Trust in the Lord with all your heart and lean not on your own understanding; in all your ways acknowledge him and he will make your paths straight.

Romans 4:21
...being fully persuaded that God had power to do what he had promised.

I Peter 5:6-7
Humble yourselves, therefore, under God's mighty hand, that he may lift you up in due time. Cast all your anxiety on him because he cares for you.

Without warning, a furious storm came
upon the lake, so that the waves
swept over the boat.....

Matthew 8:24

The lake storm arose without warning! Isn't that also the way with most life-storms? No beforehand announcement, no warning! Our first human reaction is always fear of the worst. The terrified disciples awoke a sleeping Jesus with their cry, "Save us, we are going to drown!" And, Savior that He is, He answered their plea but challenged them once again for having "little faith". Do I react to crisis with fear or faith?

The disciples had already witnessed Jesus' power to heal. Now, in the boat at Jesus' invitation, they saw Him demonstrate His power over the natural elements. Times of adversity can teach us to look immediately to Jesus, even if we are fearful or afraid. The quicker we bring Jesus into the trouble, the more we train our faith muscles to trust Him.

Jesus rebuked the waves and wind; the storm was calmed. Psalm 107 (KJV) speaks beautifully of the importance of having Jesus in your boat and crying out to Him: *They that go down to the sea in ships....these see the works of the Lord, his wonders in the deep...the stormy wind... the constant up and down of the waves...they are at their wit's end. Then they cry unto the Lord in their trouble, and he brings them out of their distresses. He makes the storm calm, so that the waves are still.*

In your life-storm, whatever is battering your boat, do not make prayer your last resort....make it your first line of defense. In your distress, cry out to the Lord. He knows about the storm. He hears, He cares, He calms. Praise God for His wonderful works to us and for us when our crisis response is to trust and thank Him.

THANK GOD: Psalm 89:8-9 ▪ Psalm 91:1-2 ▪ Jeremiah 33:3
TRUST GOD: Isaiah 41:10 ▪ Psalm 65:5,7 ▪ Psalm 107:28-31

Thank God:

Psalm 89:8-9
Who is like you, Lord God Almighty? You, Lord, are mighty, and your faithfulness surrounds you. You rule over the surging sea; when its waves mount up, you still them.

Psalm 91:1-2
Whoever dwells in the shelter of the Most High will rest in the shadow of the Almighty. I will say of the Lord, "He is my refuge and my fortress, my God, in whom I trust."

Jeremiah 33:3
Call to me and I will answer you and tell you great and unsearchable things you do not know.

Trust God:

Isaiah 41:10
So do not fear, for I am with you; do not be dismayed, for I am your God. I will strengthen you and help you; I will uphold you with my righteous right hand.

Psalm 65:5, 7
You answer us with awesome and righteous deeds, God our Savior, the hope of all the ends of the earth and of the farthest seas, who stilled the roaring of the seas, the roaring of their waves, and the turmoil of the nations.

Psalm 107:28-31
Then they cried out to the Lord in their trouble, and he brought them out of their distress. He stilled the storm to a whisper; the waves of the sea were hushed. They were glad when it grew calm, and he guided them to their desired haven. Let them give thanks to the Lord for his unfailing love and his wonderful deeds for mankind.

*Who has understood the mind of the Lord, or
instructed him as his counselor?*

Isaiah 40:13

Scripture tells us that God's understanding is unsearchable. God's thoughts are higher than our thoughts; they are *past finding out*. We simply cannot fathom how God's all-loving, all-wise ways operate when daily we see so much evidence of evil, pain, and sorrow.

My lack of knowledge and understanding humbles me; but God shows me what I can know now from Scripture and experience. From the man born blind, healed by Jesus in John 9... *One thing I do know, I was blind but now I see!* From the apostle Paul in Romans 8... *We know that all things work together for good to those that love God, to those who are called according to his purpose.* (KJV) From Paul to Timothy in II Timothy 1... *I know whom I have believed. And I am persuaded that He is able to keep that which I have committed to him against that day.* (KJV) From the suffering Job... *I know that my Redeemer lives, and that in the end He will stand upon the earth.*

For now we know in part; only later will we more fully know our Lord. For now, we know whom we have believed, and we sing songs about the wonder of what we do not yet understand: "I know not how this saving faith to me He did impart, / nor how believing in His Word wrought peace within my heart. / I know not how the Spirit moves convincing men of sin, / revealing Jesus through the Word, creating faith in Him." * The more we know of God's Word the more we learn of His ways. Though we cannot always trace Him, we can always trust Him.

THANK GOD: Isaiah 40:28 ▪ Romans 8:28-29 ▪ Colossians 1:16-17
TRUST GOD: Isaiah 55:9 ▪ Romans 11:33-34 ▪ I Corinthians 13:9,12

* Hymn, "I Know Whom I Have Believed," by Daniel W. Whittle (1883)

Thank God:

Isaiah 40:28
Do you not know? Have you not heard? The Lord is the everlasting God, the Creator of the ends of the earth. He will not grow tired or weary, and his understanding no one can fathom.

Romans 8:28-29
And we know that in all things God works for the good of those who love him, who have been called according to his purpose. For those God foreknew he also predestined to be conformed to the image of his Son, that he might be the firstborn among many brothers and sisters.

Colossians 1:16-17
For in him all things were created: things in heaven and on earth, visible and invisible, whether thrones or powers or rulers or authorities; all things have been created through him and for him. He is before all things, and in him all things hold together.

Trust God:

Isaiah 55:9
As the heavens are higher than the earth, so are my ways higher than your ways and my thoughts than your thoughts.

Romans 11:33-34
Oh, the depth of the riches of the wisdom and knowledge of God! How unsearchable his judgments, and his paths beyond tracing out! "Who has known the mind of the Lord? Or who has been his counselor?"

I Corinthians 13:9, 12
For we know in part and we prophesy in part...

For now we see only a reflection as in a mirror; then we shall see face to face. Now I know in part; then I shall know fully, even as I am fully known.

As the heavens are higher than the earth,
so are my ways higher than your ways,
and my thoughts than your thoughts.

Isaiah 55:9

"The Christian life has not been tried and found wanting. It has been found difficult and left untried." That might well have been G.K. Chesterton's opening sentence for a sermon on how much higher God's ways are than our ways. No life is long enough or deep enough to discover all the ways of the Lord; so how can we mortals know what God's higher ways are? Only by knowing, obeying, and applying what He shows us in the Holy Scripture can we ever begin to grasp His principles for living. Ironic and radical as His precepts seem to this world, God knows when our heart's desire is to try to live them out for His glory.

Ponder God's truths, consider His higher ways: Who but God could offer strength through weakness, prosperity through generosity, leadership through servanthood, significance through selflessness, rights through relinquishment, inward renewal through outward wasting, exaltation through humility, eternal life through His Son's death, and a world view where what is seen is temporary, and what is unseen is eternal.... where what we reap is what we sowed; where fear of the Lord overcomes the fear of the world?

Are you feeling helpless or hopeless about trying to live out God's higher thoughts and ways? Humanly speaking, none can do it. But our Sovereign God knows us, loves us, and will enable us as we seek to live His way....*not by might, nor by power, but by my Spirit.* (Zechariah 4:6) *For it is God who works in us both to will and to do His good pleasure.* (Philippians 2:13)

THANK GOD: Psalm 103:17-18 ▪ Galatians 6:7-9 ▪ Zechariah 4:6
TRUST GOD: II Corinthians 4:16,18; 12:9 ▪ I Peter 5:6-7 ▪ Proverbs 11:24

Thank God:

Psalm 103:17-18
But from everlasting to everlasting the Lord's love is with those who fear him, and his righteousness with their children's children—with those who keep his covenant and remember to obey his precepts.

Galatians 6:7-9
Do not be deceived: God cannot be mocked. A man reaps what he sows. Whoever sows to please their flesh, from the flesh will reap destruction; whoever sows to please the Spirit, from the Spirit will reap eternal life. Let us not become weary in doing good, for at the proper time we will reap a harvest if we do not give up.

Zechariah 4:6
So he said to me, "This is the word of the Lord to Zerubbabel: 'Not by might nor by power, but by my Spirit,' says the Lord Almighty."

Trust God:

II Corinthians 4:16, 18; 12:9
Therefore we do not lose heart. Though outwardly we are wasting away, yet inwardly we are being renewed day by day.

So we fix our eyes not on what is seen, but on what is unseen, since what is seen is temporary, but what is unseen is eternal.

But he said to me, "My grace is sufficient for you, for my power is made perfect in weakness." Therefore I will boast all the more gladly about my weaknesses, so that Christ's power may rest on me.

I Peter 5:6-7
Humble yourselves, therefore, under God's mighty hand, that he may lift you up in due time. Cast all your anxiety on him because he cares for you.

Proverbs 11:24
One person gives freely, yet gains even more; another withholds unduly, but comes to poverty.

*Do not store up for yourselves
treasures on earth....
But store up for yourselves
treasures in heaven....
where your treasure is, there will
your heart be also.*

Matthew 6:19-21

Few experiences are more thrilling than the discovery of treasure. The lifetime work of marine salvage operators is searching the ocean depths for sunken treasure. Hikers armed with metal detectors scan the earth for bits of lost or hidden treasure. Miners risk everything to find underground veins of gold and silver or rocks with pockets of valuable gems. Some treasures are discovered by accident; others are found by a deliberately planned search and determined perseverance. The goal of the hunt is always reward.

God's perspective on treasure differs from ours. The riches involved are spiritual, not monetary. Jesus taught his followers not to store up treasures on earth, but to store up "treasures in heaven." That does not mean you should not enjoy a hunt for earthly treasures. The question is what your heart is set on....God's eternal perspective or an immediate gain of wealth or power? Psalm 19 speaks of God's precepts and statutes as more precious then gold, and assures us that *in keeping them, there is great reward.*

The Scriptures speak of Christ, *in whom are hidden all the treasures of wisdom and knowledge.* The apostle Paul wanted believers to *have the full riches of complete understanding, that they might know the mystery of God, namely, Christ Jesus.* Do you know Him as Savior and Lord? Have you ever thought of mining for gems and nuggets in God's word? Knowledge, wisdom and understanding of the Lord's words and ways are riches no one can steal away from the heart that treasures them. *Oh, the depth of the riches of the wisdom and knowledge of God!* Search for your treasure in God's word!

THANK GOD: Psalm 19:8-11 ▪ Colossians 2:2-3 ▪ Romans 11:33
TRUST GOD: Job 23:12 ▪ Psalm 45:3 ▪ Proverbs 22:4

Thank God:

Psalm 19:8-11
The precepts of the Lord are right, giving joy to the heart. The commands of the Lord are radiant, giving light to the eyes. The fear of the Lord is pure, enduring forever. The decrees of the Lord are firm, and all of them are righteous. They are more precious than gold, than much pure gold; they are sweeter than honey, than honey from the honeycomb. By them your servant is warned; in keeping them there is great reward.

Colossians 2:2-3
My goal is that they may be encouraged in heart and united in love, so that they may have the full riches of complete understanding, in order that they may know the mystery of God, namely, Christ, in whom are hidden all the treasures of wisdom and knowledge.

Romans 11:33
Oh, the depth of the riches of the wisdom and knowledge of God! How unsearchable his judgments, and his paths beyond tracing out!

Trust God:

Job 23:12
I have not departed from the commands of his lips; I have treasured the words of his mouth more than my daily bread.

Psalm 45:3
Gird your sword on your side, you mighty one; clothe yourself with splendor and majesty.

Proverbs 22:4
Humility is the fear of the Lord; its wages are riches and honor and life.

.....written to teach us, so that through endurance and the encouragement of the Scriptures we might have hope.

Romans 15:4

Long distance runners know the importance of endurance. Hours of fitness training, weeks of practice runs, months of trying to beat a personal best....all add up to an endurance challenge. My mother used to say that being a champion means holding on for one minute more! When endurance is tested in a marathon, nothing becomes more important than cheers or words of encouragement from those who believe you can hold on and finish triumphantly!

Does daily life seem to be a marathon right now? A stressful job? Exhausting family duties? Struggling with a chronic illness? Serious medical treatments? Responsibilities as a single parent? If you are weary of enduring, take to heart God's invitation to read the Scriptures for encouragement and renewal of hope. God's words have the power to strengthen body, mind, and spirit in a way that self-help alone cannot. Your Creator knows the race you are in, and His strengthening will encourage endurance and hope. Believe God for the truth of His words; secure your hope by reading Scripture. Read it, believe it, then follow God's word and *run with patience the race* set before you, *looking unto Jesus, the author and finisher of our faith....who for the joy that was set before Him endured the cross...* Have you ever looked to Jesus to sustain you? Seek Him who endured the cross for you. He is your help and hope to finish your life marathon, not just somehow, but triumphantly!

THANK GOD: Psalm 119:14 ▪ Isaiah 40:8,31 ▪ Philippians 4:13,19
TRUST GOD: Romans 15:5 ▪ II Corinthians 4:17-18 ▪ Hebrews 12:1-2

Thank God:

Psalm 119:14
I rejoice in following your statutes as one rejoices in great riches.

Isaiah 40:8, 31
The grass withers and the flowers fall, but the word of our God stands for-ever....those who hope in the Lord will renew their strength.

Philippians 4:13, 19
I can do everything through him who gives me strength. And my God will meet all your needs according to his glorious riches in Christ Jesus.

Trust God:

Romans 15:5
May the God who gives endurance and encouragement give you a spirit of unity among yourselves as you follow Christ Jesus...

II Corinthians 4:17-18
For our light and momentary troubles are achieving for us an eternal glory that far outweighs them all. So we fix our eyes not on what is seen, but on what is unseen. For what is seen is temporary, but what is unseen is eternal.

Hebrews 12:1-2
...let us throw off everything that hinders and the sin that so easily entan-gles, and let us run with perseverance the race marked out for us. Let us fix our eyes on Jesus, the author and finisher of our faith, who for the joy that was set before him endured the cross, scorning the shame, and sat down at the right hand of the throne of God.

No eye has seen, no ear has heard, no mind has conceived what God has prepared for those who love him.

I Corinthians 2:9

God is good all the time, but amazingly, He is always better than we know. He loves to gift our eyes with a spectacular view of His Creation. He brings to our ears inspiring music or news seemingly out of the blue that is thrilling to hear. Our minds may receive new insights on dreams we have longed for, waited for, even prayed for. Specific moments from God for those who love Him and depend on His grace are a testimony to His amazing goodness! Our challenge is to resist measuring God's power by our own meager abilities. His "unfathomable wonders and countless miracles" fuel our hope and convince us to trust Him for His best in our lives....to watch and listen for His personalized providences.

In The God of All Comfort, Hannah W. Smith asks whether "our God has been over-advertised and our Savior over-estimated?" She answers with a resounding "No." We have, instead, "under-believed and under-trusted the Triune God, in whom we live and move and have our being." Feeling weak? Ask God to strengthen you in hope, in courage, in stamina, in confidence. Out of resources? Ask God to supply your lack. *The earth is the Lord's and everything in it.* He is the ultimate dream weaver, working for us behind the scenes. Confused, perplexed, indecisive? Ask the Spirit to guide you with His counsel, to open and close doors for you, to show you God's best choices. Remember God's invitation to call upon Him. He will show you the inconceivable things, far better than you know, that He has prepared for His beloved!

THANK GOD: Psalm 24:1 ▪ Isaiah 64:4 ▪ Acts 17:27-28
TRUST GOD: Job 5:9, 9:10 ▪ Psalm 73:24 ▪ Jeremiah 32:27, 33:3

Thank God:

Psalm 24:1
The earth is the Lord's, and everything in it, the world, and all who live in it...

Isaiah 64:4
Since ancient times no one has heard, no ear has perceived, no eye has seen any God besides you, who acts on behalf of those who wait for him.

Acts 17:27-28
God did this so that they would seek him and perhaps reach out for him and find him, though he is not far from any one of us. "For in him we live and move and have our being." As some of your own poets have said, "We are his offspring."

Trust God:

Job 5:9, 9:10
He performs wonders that cannot be fathomed, miracles that cannot be counted.

Psalm 73:24
You guide me with your counsel, and afterward you will take me into glory.

Jeremiah 32:27, 33:3
I am the Lord, the God of all mankind. Is anything too hard for me?

Call to me and I will answer you and tell you great and unsearchable things you do not know.

*Thou shalt not take the name of the
Lord thy God in vain.*

Exodus 20:7 Deuteronomy 5:11 KJV

Today the names of God and Jesus Christ are heard twice as much in cursing as in praying. In the marketplace, in movies, on television, in conversation, the Lord's name is constantly misused....expressing amazement or surprise, horror, disdain, disgust, or damnation. The third of the Ten Commandments, given to Moses by God as His law of behavior, speech and conduct, forbids the irreverent use of His name. *Do not profane my holy name* is a recurring command in Scripture. God warns us to guard our tongue, to think before we speak, so we will not malign and impugn God's name. Indeed, the third commandment continues....*the Lord will not hold anyone guiltless who misuses his name.*

When Jesus gave the disciples a model prayer, He began with, *Our Father, who art in heaven, hallowed be thy name.* Because He is a Holy God, His name is holy. Yet He graciously invites His followers to call on His name for daily bread, for forgiveness, for deliverance from evil. Misusing or abusing God's name not only dishonors Him, but may blind us to blessings associated with revering it. *The name of the Lord is a strong tower; the righteous run to it and are safe.* Jesus' name is *the name above all names,* the name before which *every knee will bow....*the only name under heaven by which anyone may be saved for eternity. The power of His name is a basis for hope; so let us glorify the Lord and exalt His name together. Let us hope in His name, not use it in vain.

THANK GOD: Psalm 115:1 ▪ Proverbs 18:10 ▪ Philippians 2:9-11
TRUST GOD: Leviticus 20:7, 22:31 ▪ Acts 4:12, 10:45 ▪ Colossians 3:17

Thank God:

Psalm 115:1
Not to us, Lord, not to us but to your name be the glory, because of your love and faithfulness.

Proverbs 18:10
The name of the Lord is a fortified tower; the righteous run to it and are safe.

Philippians 2:9-11
Therefore God exalted him to the highest place and gave him the name that is above every name, that at the name of Jesus every knee should bow, in heaven and on earth and under the earth, and every tongue acknowledge that Jesus Christ is Lord, to the glory of God the Father.

Trust God:

Leviticus 20:7, 22:31
Consecrate yourselves and be holy, because I am the Lord your God.

Keep my commands and follow them. I am the Lord.

Acts 4:12, 10:45
Salvation is found in no one else, for there is no other name under heaven given to mankind by which we must be saved.

The circumcised believers who had come with Peter were astonished that the gift of the Holy Spirit had been poured out even on Gentiles.

Colossians 3:17
And whatever you do, whether in word or deed, do it all in the name of the Lord Jesus, giving thanks to God the Father through him.

Devote yourselves to prayer, being
watchful and thankful.

Colossians 4:2

Following the death of a friend or loved one, we often hear or say that he or she lived "a full life." Perhaps we will talk about their natural talents and abilities, their memberships or special accomplishments. But Scripture reveals other ways to assess the fullness of a life....ways that God's word commends to our hearts, if or when we might want to self-evaluate the "fullness" of our own lives. Colossians 4 gives us words of "fullness" by which a life can honor God and serve others. To be devoted to prayer is to be <u>prayerful</u>, while also being <u>watchful</u> and <u>thankful</u>. Do you watch for ways to thank God for His love shown in a situation or to trust Him for His power to intervene on someone's behalf? To be <u>careful</u> not only means being cautious, but aware and concerned about another's problems or needs. The admonition in 4:6 is to let your conversation be <u>graceful</u>, *always full of grace.* Let your talk be <u>tasteful</u>, *seasoned with salt*, and <u>helpful</u>, *always ready to give an answer to everyone*....a <u>truthful</u> answer, of course! Not a lot of small talk in these encounters!

A full life is a <u>faithful</u> life, for *without faith it is impossible to please God.* Believe God for His promises, and honor His word. Being <u>joyful</u> is possible because the God of Hope fills us with joy and peace as we trust in Him. The fullness of your life depends not on your age, or your prominence, or particular achievements, but on a desire to please God....to fulfill His standards for fullness of the *life that is truly life.*

THANK GOD: Romans 15:13 ▪ I Thessalonians 5:17 ▪ Hebrews 4:16
TRUST GOD: Philippians 4:6 ▪ I Timothy 6:18-19 ▪ Hebrews 11:6

Thank God:

Romans 15:13
May the God of hope fill you with all joy and peace as you trust in him, so that you may overflow with hope by the power of the Holy Spirit.

I Thessalonians 5:17
...pray continually...

Hebrews 4:16
Let us then approach God's throne of grace with confidence, so that we may receive mercy and find grace to help us in our time of need.

Trust God:

Philippians 4:6
Do not be anxious about anything, but in every situation, by prayer and petition, with thanksgiving, present your requests to God.

I Timothy 6:18-19
Command them to do good, to be rich in good deeds, and to be generous and willing to share. In this way they will lay up treasure for themselves as a firm foundation for the coming age, so that they may take hold of the life that is truly life.

Hebrews 11:6
And without faith it is impossible to please God, because anyone who comes to him must believe that he exists and that he rewards those who earnestly seek him.

.....He leads me beside quiet waters,
He restores my soul.

Psalm 23:2

Often tagged the Psalm of the Good Shepherd, Psalm 23 begins "The Lord is my shepherd, I shall not want." Having no wants is a true statement of hope! Water, food and protection are the primary needs a shepherd must provide. Sheep drink deepest from still waters, not from rocky rapids or dangerous currents. Safe sheep learn to follow the voice of their shepherd as he moves them to greener pastures to find plentiful nourishment. Jesus calls Himself our good Shepherd. He knows we need even more care than the wool-bearing animals. We need that time, that place beside still waters, for restoration of a fainting soul and a refreshment of faith in His provisions and plans for us.

The tyranny of technology and the pace of life today create a contrast to God's best for us. As rafters on roaring rapids can hardly hear one another's voices, we often cannot hear His words: *Be still and know that I am God. Be still before the Lord and wait patiently for Him.* Stillness and patience invite God's renewal. Striving to be seen, to be heard, to labor in self-sovereignty flies in the face of a soul at rest.

Praying for restoration of soul, one Psalmist repeats his prayer three times, increasingly emphasizing the Lord Himself, the source of restoration. Psalm 80 records his first call: *Restore us, O God*; then he prays again: *Restore us, O God, Almighty*; his final plea is *Restore us, O Lord God, Almighty, make your face shine upon us, that we may be saved.* Our good shepherd is our Savior!

THANK GOD: Psalm 46:10 ▪ Isaiah 30:15 ▪ John 10:3-5,11,14
TRUST GOD: Psalm 37:7 ▪ Psalm 51:12 ▪ Psalm 80:3,7,19

Thank God:

Psalm 46:10
He says, "Be still, and know that I am God; I will be exalted among the nations, I will be exalted in the earth."

Isaiah 30:15
This is what the Sovereign Lord, the Holy One of Israel, says: "In repentance and rest is your salvation, in quietness and trust is your strength, but you would have none of it."

John 10:3-5, 11, 14
The gatekeeper opens the gate for him, and the sheep listen to his voice. He calls his own sheep by name and leads them out. When he has brought out all his own, he goes on ahead of them, and his sheep follow him because they know his voice. But they will never follow a stranger; in fact, they will run away from him because they do not recognize a stranger's voice.

I am the good shepherd. The good shepherd lays down his life for the sheep.

I am the good shepherd; I know my sheep and my sheep know me...

Trust God:

Psalm 37:7
Be still before the Lord and wait patiently for him; do not fret when people succeed in their ways, when they carry out their wicked schemes.

Psalm 51:12
Restore to me the joy of your salvation and grant me a willing spirit, to sustain me.

Psalm 80:3, 7, 19
Restore us, O God; make your face shine on us, that we may be saved.

*Ascribe to the Lord the glory due His name;
worship the Lord in the splendor of
his holiness.*

Psalm 29:2

Holy, holy, holy is the Lord God Almighty.

Isaiah 6:3 Revelation 4:8

God teaches Israel from the beginning that above all He is holy....*majestic in holiness, awesome in glory, working wonders.* His holiness means His presence makes places holy: the mountain where God called to Moses from a burning bush, the Holy of Holies in the traveling tabernacle and later in the Temple where only the High Priest could enter to seek atonement for Israel's sins. The holiness of God stands in contrast to human sinfulness. The Lord never let Israel forget that He is holy and must be approached with reverential awe. Yet He invites and desires His people to come to Him for redemption and a personal relationship with the Creator, our Father in heaven, immortal and invisible. The *splendor of His holiness* demands a silent reverence before Him in worship, coupled with joyful singing to the glory of His name, providing witness to a victorious faith in Him.

God still calls His people to be holy. A God who is worthy of worship and praise may sound unapproachable to those who already know themselves to be unholy. But remember God's gift to the world He so loved was His son, Jesus, the Redeemer of all sin and ungodliness. When you place a thankful, personal faith and trust in Jesus, God's Spirit creates a desire to seek a holy life by His grace and purpose. *Be holy, because I am holy.* Lord, let that be my heart's desire today.

THANK GOD: Exodus 3:4-6 ▪ Leviticus 11:45 ▪ Habakkuk 2:20
TRUST GOD: Exodus 15:11 ▪ John 1:14 ▪ I Peter 1:15-16

Thank God:

Exodus 3:4-6
When the Lord saw that he had gone over to look, God called to him from within the bush, "Moses! Moses!" And Moses said, "Here I am." "Do not come any closer," God said. "Take off your sandals, for the place where you are standing is holy ground." Then he said, "I am the God of your father, the God of Abraham, the God of Isaac and the God of Jacob." At this, Moses hid his face, because he was afraid to look at God.

Leviticus 11:45
I am the Lord, who brought you up out of Egypt to be your God; therefore be holy, because I am holy.

Habakkuk 2:20
The Lord is in his holy temple; let all the earth be silent before him.

Trust God:

Exodus 15:11
Who among the gods is like you, Lord? Who is like you—majestic in holiness, awesome in glory, working wonders?

John 1:14
The Word became flesh and made his dwelling among us. We have seen his glory, the glory of the one and only Son, who came from the Father, full of grace and truth.

I Peter 1:15-16
But just as he who called you is holy, so be holy in all you do; for it is written: "Be holy, because I am holy."

Your love has given me great joy and encouragement because you, brother, have refreshed the hearts of the saints.

Philemon 7

Love, joy, encouragement, refreshment....could there be any better harbingers of revival or renewal of hope? Even the Apostle Paul, who had "learned to be content," (Philippians 4:12) was blessed by his fellow worker's loving, refreshing encouragements. Those serving others will always benefit from a thankful or positive word. If you have been fortunate enough to have a cheerleader among your associates, you know the uplifting effect of specific, personal affirmation.

The concept of being "blest to be a blessing" is not just a New Testament truth. A very wise king nearly a thousand years before Christ observed a similar phenomena, recording in Proverbs: *he who refreshes others will himself be refreshed.* Like sowing and reaping, refreshment and hope result when we demonstrate our love for God by loving and appreciating another....whether by word or deed.

Do you know someone who could use refreshment? Maybe a personal word of encouragement to one doing a menial job well....or a written expression of appreciation for extra work done without grumbling! If you are a leader or officer over many employees, have you ever called by name someone who had no idea you even knew it? Have you acknowledged with a smile one who might be fighting a personal battle on another front? One lady enjoyed anonymously prepaying for the lunch of a soldier in line somewhere behind her, with instructions to say only "thank you for your service to this nation." Today, why not find words of thanks or deeds of appreciation to surprise a co-worker, a service man or woman, a first responder, pastor, teacher, friend, or family member? You could be the one surprised at who gets the most joy and satisfaction from the endeavor!

THANK GOD: Proverbs 11:25 ▪ Proverbs 12:25 ▪ Proverbs 22:9
TRUST GOD: Romans 1:11-12 ▪ Galatians 6:9-10 ▪ II Thessalonians 2:16-17

Thank God:

Proverbs 11:25
A generous person will prosper; whoever refreshes others will be refreshed.

Proverbs 12:25
Anxiety weighs down the heart, but a kind word cheers it up.

Proverbs 22:9
The generous will themselves be blessed, for they share their food with the poor.

Trust God:

Romans 1:11-12
I long to see you so that I may impart to you some spiritual gift to make you strong—that is, that you and I may be mutually encouraged by each other's faith.

Galatians 6:9-10
Let us not become weary in doing good, for at the proper time we will reap a harvest if we do not give up. Therefore, as we have opportunity, let us do good to all people, especially to those who belong to the family of believers.

II Thessalonians 2:16-17
May our Lord Jesus Christ himself and God our Father, who loved us and by his grace gave us eternal encouragement and good hope, encourage your hearts and strengthen you in every good deed and word.

But I trust in you, O Lord. I say,
"You are My God."
My times are in your hands.

Psalm 31:14-15

In <u>Gulliver's Travels,</u> when Gulliver is captured by the Lilliputians, the tiny men notice he keeps looking at his watch. They begin to wonder if it is his god because he is always consulting it.* Today, a hand-held or wrist-mounted technologic wonder might be considered the god of the 21ˢᵗ century, demanding constant attention. Indeed, time and contact are huge factors of life on earth. Productive lives depend on precise scheduling with instant communications. But how then can we face the tyranny of technology without making it our master or a god?

The Psalmist humbly tells the Lord, "My times are in your hands." Ultimately, God is in control, sovereign over the time and "the times" of our lives. Only He knows the best use and arrangement of the hours in our day. We may seek to be wise with the time given to us, but plans can change, even in an instant. Poet Robert Burns coined this reality in his famous line: "The best laid plans of mice and men often go awry...." And a C.S. Lewis wise word advises all to "write your plans in pencil so God can change them at His will." That advice acknowledges and honors our Sovereign God, with cooperative stewardship, flexibility, and priorities.

Have you considered putting your schedule or hourly calendar before God in prayer, asking Him to change or rearrange anything not His best for you that day? Tell the Lord <u>He</u> is your God, your trust, not a watch or a mobile device. Whether or not He changes anything, He will honor your trust in Him, and His plans are always better than you could ask or think!

THANK GOD: Isaiah 33:6 ▪ Daniel 2:21 ▪ Ephesians 3:20
TRUST GOD: Psalm 62:8 ▪ Proverbs 16:9 ▪ Jeremiah 17:7

* Charles Colson, BreakPoint Radio

Thank God:

Isaiah 33:6
He will be the sure foundation for your times, a rich store of salvation and wisdom and knowledge; the fear of the Lord is the key to this treasure.

Daniel 2:21
He changes times and seasons; he deposes kings and raises up others. He gives wisdom to the wise and knowledge to the discerning.

Ephesians 3:20
Now to him who is able to do immeasurably more than all we ask or imagine, according to his power that is at work within us...

Trust God:

Psalm 62:8
Trust in him at all times, you people; pour out your hearts to him, for God is our refuge.

Proverbs 16:9
In their hearts humans plan their course, but the Lord establishes their steps.

Jeremiah 17:7
But blessed is the one who trusts in the Lord, whose confidence is in him.

*God has said, "Never will I leave you;
never will I forsake you."*

Hebrews 13:5

*And surely I am with you always, to the
very end of the age.*

Matthew 28:20

Two words <u>only</u> God can say in total truthfulness are NEVER and ALWAYS. Promises of men, women, sisters, brothers, husbands and wives are often broken. Fickleness dilutes truthfulness. Hypocrisy can only pretend to be truthful. The selfishness of our affections leads to unkept promises. No wonder we fear that no one can be trusted.

If you have been betrayed by broken promises or vows, seek God's words of comfort and reassurance from the Scriptures. <u>Never</u> is our Lord untruthful. His word stands true forever....we can believe it, count on it, and come into His presence confidently with it, singing with John Newton: "The Lord has promised good to me; His word my hope secures." Believe the Bible's words of hope: God, the Father, <u>never</u> forsakes, and Jesus, His Son, our Savior, confirms He will be with us <u>always</u>! When we are desperate for God's encouragement and help, we can stand on His promises. Commit to Him your need for hope.

Hopelessness can lead to a sense of abandonment, but no matter the reason for that feeling, fix your heart to believe God's words of comfort for you. He is a father to the fatherless, a defender of widows, a refuge for the lonely or estranged, a provider for the poor, and a stronghold in the day of trouble. Trust our powerful, loving God for the truth of His words....NEVER and ALWAYS!

THANK GOD: Deuteronomy 31:6 ▪ Isaiah 40:8 ▪ Nahum 1:7
TRUST GOD: Psalm 31:7,14,16,24 ▪ Psalm 68:5 ▪ Psalm 119:89-90,114

Thank God:

Deuteronomy 31:6
Be strong and courageous. Do not be afraid or terrified because of them, for the Lord your God goes with you; he will never leave you nor forsake you.

Isaiah 40:8
The grass withers and the flowers fall, but the word of our God endures forever.

Nahum 1:7
The Lord is good, a refuge in times of trouble. He cares for those who trust in him...

Trust God:

Psalm 31:7, 14, 16, 24
I will be glad and rejoice in your love, for you saw my affliction and knew the anguish of my soul.

But I trust in you, Lord; I say, "You are my God."

Let your face shine on your servant; save me in your unfailing love.

Be strong and take heart, all you who hope in the Lord.

Psalm 68:5
A father to the fatherless, a defender of widows, is God in his holy dwelling.

Psalm 119:89-90, 114
Your word, Lord, is eternal; it stands firm in the heavens. Your faithfulness continues through all generations; you established the earth, and it endures.

You are my refuge and my shield; I have put my hope in your word.

Who despises the day of small things?

Zechariah 4:10

Ever feel like a speck of dust in the starry universe? Does daily life seem unimportant, insignificant? Are you wishing you could do "big things" for God, for others? Rejoice! A sense of smallness makes it more likely that you will take refuge in God, praying in humility for the Holy Spirit to give you an "opportunity for usefulness." (Puritan Prayers) "Find out what God would thee do, and do that little well. For what is great and what is small, 'tis only He can tell." (Anonymous)

Mother Teresa's counsel was not to do "great things" for God, but "small things with much love for a great God." Are you laboring unappreciated, underpaid? Offer your hard work to God. Are you on a perpetual professional treadmill? Pray for excellence and accuracy in your work. Ask God for a wisdom that sets you apart. Are your hopes limited because of health, a handicap, or scarce financial resources? Ask the Lord to give you an opportunity for impact in some area of your life.

Susanna Wesley, remarkable 18th century English wife and mother, taught all her children to cry softly and home-schooled thirteen of them, teaching all to read and counseling each on living a holy life. Sons John and Charles went on to Oxford University, becoming priests and song-writers in the Anglican Church. Susanna had a sense of selflessness that was humbly expressed in her life message: "I am content to fill a little space, if God be glorified." Despise not small beginnings, small places, small spaces. Remember that nothing is small if God is in it....because great is His power and great is His faithfulness!

THANK GOD: Zechariah 4:6 ▪ Matthew 25:21 ▪ Ephesians 2:10
TRUST GOD: I Samuel 16:7 ▪ Philippians 4:12-13 ▪ I Timothy 4:12

Thank God:

Zechariah 4:6
So he said to me, "This is the word of the Lord to Zerubbabel: 'Not by might nor by power, but by my Spirit,' says the Lord Almighty."

Matthew 25:21
His master replied, "Well done, good and faithful servant! You have been faithful with a few things; I will put you in charge of many things. Come and share your master's happiness!"

Ephesians 2:10
For we are God's handiwork, created in Christ Jesus to do good works, which God prepared in advance for us to do.

Trust God:

I Samuel 16:7
But the Lord said to Samuel, "Do not consider his appearance or his height, for I have rejected him. The Lord does not look at the things people look at. People look at the outward appearance, but the Lord looks at the heart."

Philippians 4:12-13
I know what it is to be in need, and I know what it is to have plenty. I have learned the secret of being content in any and every situation, whether well fed or hungry, whether living in plenty or in want. I can do all this through him who gives me strength.

I Timothy 4:12
Don't let anyone look down on you because you are young, but set an example for the believers in speech, in conduct, in love, in faith and in purity.

For the eyes of the Lord are on the righteous and His ears are attentive to their prayer.....

I Peter 3:12

Our Sovereign God is all-seeing, all-knowing, ever present. Yet Scripture ascribes to Him features common to human beings created in His image. His <u>ears</u> are open and attentive to our cries and prayers. In His <u>hand</u> He holds the heart of a king and can turn it however He wills. His <u>voice</u> calls His sheep by name but warns against a hardening of heart when we hear His call. And His amazing <u>eyes</u> keep watch on those who fear Him and hope in His unfailing love....reminding us that man looks at outward appearances, but God sees into our heart....no matter where we are or what our situation is.

Have ever found yourself in a spot where you realized no one but God knew where you were at that moment? Survival stories from former hostages, prisoners of war, and lost solo travelers are usually laced with humble thanks for the knowledge of God's unfailing love and presence to sustain their strength, endurance, and hope. One year during an onshore excursion from a cruise ship, I had a small, all-alone experience. Our vehicle had traversed rough, rocky roads into the remote hinterland of an impoverished island. Any conversation was difficult as most of the group did not speak English. We climbed the heights to a river-rafting launch. Alone on a rickety, bamboo raft steered by a strange pole man, I lost sight of the other rafts as we moved down the river. God was my refuge, my protection, and my hope for a safe, timely return. How thankful I was then and now for His all-seeing eyes and prayer-hearing ears!

THANK GOD: Psalm 34:7,17 ▪ Psalm 147:11 ▪ Proverbs 21:1
TRUST GOD: Psalm 91:14-15 ▪ Psalm 95:7-8 ▪ Proverbs 15:3

Thank God:

Psalm 34:7, 17
The angel of the Lord encamps around those who fear him, and he delivers them.

The righteous cry out, and the Lord hears them; he delivers them from all their troubles.

Psalm 147:11
...the Lord delights in those who fear him, who put their hope in his unfailing love.

Proverbs 21:1
In the Lord's hand the king's heart is a stream of water that he channels toward all who please him.

Trust God:

Psalm 91:14-15
"Because he loves me," says the Lord, "I will rescue him; I will protect him, for he acknowledges my name. He will call on me, and I will answer him; I will be with him in trouble, I will deliver him and honor him."

Psalm 95:7-8
...for he is our God and we are the people of his pasture, the flock under his care. Today, if only you would hear his voice, "Do not harden your hearts as you did at Meribah, as you did that day at Massah in the wilderness..."

Proverbs 15:3
The eyes of the Lord are everywhere, keeping watch on the wicked and the good.

This is the day the Lord has made; let us rejoice and be glad in it.

Psalm 118:24

As an out-of-town grandmother, I used to call ahead to my grandchildren's house upon leaving the airport en route to see them. On one visit my young grandson surprised me with his animated response on the phone, "Oh, Grammy, I can't wait to see what you have brought me!" How's that for pressure? And yet, I loved that he associated me with giving. I soon realized I should have the same excited expectancy for my heavenly Father every morning when He gives me a new day… "Lord, I can't wait to see what you have for me today!" Each day can begin with joy in expectancy and hope.

The future belongs to God. We cannot arrange it, so how can we rejoice and be glad in each day when we do not know its outcome? Our confidence is in God's word: He knows what we need before we ask, and He knows those who are trusting and thanking Him. And since we know that His mercies are new every morning, let us arise, open to God's gifts of love, grace, adventure, merriment, even challenge.

Whatever our day, whatever our need, whatever our situation, God knows, He cares, He provides, and He sustains. Even though we do not know what the day will bring forth or how God may surprise us, we can rest on His sovereignty. He has the power to make good on His promise that ALL things can work together for good in the lives of those who love Him and are called by Him. So rise and shine, rejoice and be glad….the Lord has brought you and me a new day!

THANK GOD: Matthew 6:8 ▪ II Corinthians 9:8 ▪ Psalm 68:3
TRUST GOD: Lamentations 3:22-23 ▪ Philippians 4:4,19 ▪ Romans 8:28

Thank God:

Matthew 6:8
Do not be like them, for your Father knows what you need before you ask him.

II Corinthians 9:8
And God is able to bless you abundantly, so that in all things at all times, having all that you need, you will abound in every good work.

Psalm 68:3
But may the righteous be glad and rejoice before God; may they be happy and joyful.

Trust God:

Lamentations 3:22-23
Because of the Lord's great love we are not consumed, for his compassions never fail. They are new every morning; great is your faithfulness.

Philippians 4:4, 19
Rejoice in the Lord always. I will say it again: Rejoice!

And my God will meet all your needs according to the riches of his glory in Christ Jesus.

Romans 8:28
And we know that in all things God works for the good of those who love him, who have been called according to his purpose.

The Lord delights in those who fear him,
who put their hope in his unfailing love.

Psalm 147:11

Imagine yourself being a delight to God! Our intentions should always be to please Him, but frequently efforts seem to fall short. This verse assures us of two things delighting God involves, and neither is perfection or a sterling performance. The Lord's delight is a matter of the heart: fearing Him and hoping in His unfailing love (KJV "mercy").

Do you fear God? Not are you afraid of Him, but rather do you have a belief in His existence, accompanied by an awesome reverence for His holiness and an acknowledgement of His sovereignty? Do you see the Lord as the ultimate power above all forces, all thrones, kingdoms, and rulers? If you are one who fears the Lord, pray like the Puritans for the Holy Spirit to "melt your heart by the majesty and mercy of God."

Is your hope in God's unfailing love? No more reliable place to put your hope exists than in the merciful, inexhaustible Love that sent Jesus to die to redeem sinners so they can approach a holy God without receiving His wrath. (Moses warned that God's *wrath is as great as the fear* that is due Him. Holiness and sinfulness cannot co-exist.) If you need a revival of hope at this moment, recall and sing this simple song: "Jesus loves me, this I know, for the Bible tells me so." Thank God that He wants to delight in you because you fear Him and trust His unfailing love to provide the best hope you could ever have....to live an abundant life here and now and spend Eternity in His presence!

THANK GOD: Proverbs 9:10, 19:23 ▪ Zephaniah 3:17 ▪ John 10:10 KJV
TRUST GOD: Psalm 13:5-6 ▪ Psalm 33:20-22 ▪ Psalm 90:11

Thank God:

Proverbs 9:10, 19:23
The fear of the Lord is the beginning of wisdom, and knowledge of the Holy One is understanding.

The fear of the Lord leads to life; then one rests content, untouched by trouble.

Zephaniah 3:17
The Lord your God is with you, the Mighty Warrior who saves. He will take great delight in you; in his love he will no longer rebuke you, but will rejoice over you with singing.

John 10:10 KJV
The thief cometh not, but for to steal, and to kill, and to destroy: I am come that they might have life, and that they might have it more abundantly.

Trust God:

Psalm 13:5-6
But I trust in your unfailing love; my heart rejoices in your salvation. I will sing the Lord's praise, for he has been good to me.

Psalm 33:20-22
We wait in hope for the Lord; he is our help and our shield. In him our hearts rejoice, for we trust in his holy name. May your unfailing love be with us, Lord, even as we put our hope in you.

Psalm 90:11
If only we knew the power of your anger! Your wrath is as great as the fear that is your due.

Trust in the Lord with all your heart and lean not on your own understanding....

Proverbs 3:5

Even the Biblically illiterate know something about Job. We say a friend has "the patience of Job," or "more troubles than Job," because Job's life is a metaphor for devastating trials due to circumstances beyond his control. Loss of his family, his home, and his health made it tough to hope in the goodness of God. If our life is spiraling downward, we think of ourselves as modern-day Jobs. But rarely do you hear of Job's ultimate trust in the Lord, even as he poured out his pain over what he perceived as God's lack of concern. Job held on to hope that God would eventually break His silence and affirm to Job this truth: Despite circumstances to the contrary, He is <u>The God Who Is There</u>, as Francis Schaffer would write millennia later.

Let Job's trust in the Lord encourage you with a new perspective. Incredibly, amidst his multiplying trials and losses, Job spoke these words: *"Though he slay me, <u>yet</u> will I trust him" (Job 13:15 KJV); "I know that my redeemer lives, and in the end he <u>will</u> stand upon the earth" (Job 19:25); "But he knows the way that I take; when he has tested me I <u>shall</u> come forth as gold." (Job 23:10)*

For all of the questions surrounding Job's devastating losses, few had answers. But once Job heard from the Lord Himself, the <u>shall</u>, the <u>will</u>, and the <u>yet</u> of his trust were validated. Let Job's word picture of gold purified by the fires of adversity encourage you until you hear God speak....whether in a still, small voice, a thundering shout, or a quiet whisper of His love as you read the Bible's living words about Job, whose suffering but trusting heart chose not to lean only on his own understanding, but on God Himself.

THANK GOD: Job 38:1-2, 42:1-3 ▪ Isaiah 25:8-9 ▪ II Timothy 4:18
TRUST GOD: Proverbs 14:32 ▪ Psalm 42:11 ▪ Psalm 91:15

Thank God:

Job 38:1-2, 42:1-3
Then the Lord spoke to Job out of the storm. He said: "Who is this that obscures my plans with words without knowledge?"

Then Job replied to the Lord: "I know that you can do all things; no purpose of yours can be thwarted. You asked, 'Who is this that obscures my plans without knowledge?' Surely I spoke of things I did not understand, things too wonderful for me to know."

Isaiah 25:8-9
...he will swallow up death forever. The Sovereign Lord will wipe away the tears from all faces; he will remove his people's disgrace from all the earth. The Lord has spoken. In that day they will say, "Surely this is our God; we trusted in him, and he saved us. This is the Lord, we trusted in him; let us rejoice and be glad in his salvation."

II Timothy 4:18
The Lord will rescue me from every evil attack and will bring me safely to his heavenly kingdom. To him be glory for ever and ever. Amen.

Trust God:

Proverbs 14:32
When calamity comes, the wicked are brought down, but even in death the righteous seek refuge in God.

Psalm 42:11
Why, my soul, are you downcast? Why so disturbed within me? Put your hope in God, for I will yet praise him, my Savior and my God.

Psalm 91:15
He will call on me, and I will answer him; I will be with him in trouble, I will deliver him and honor him.

O, Israel, put your hope in the Lord,
for with the Lord
is unfailing love, and with
him is full redemption.

Psalm 130:7

As God's people made a pilgrimage up to Jerusalem on festival or feast days, they would sing "songs of ascent" as they climbed, mentally and spiritually preparing themselves for worship on Mt. Zion. Praise and thanksgiving were part of the songs, but hopeful expectation was often a theme as the pilgrims cried out for mercy to the one and only Lord, God Almighty. Whether beseeching His blessing, or confessing both faith and sin, or just singing for joy, the songs of ascent can become our songs as we personalize the Psalms.

Are you, am I, waiting for the Lord and putting our hope in Him and His word? Can we really make that declaration? Instead of naming "Israel" in the above verse, insert your name and read the verse aloud. Tell your heart you do put your hope in the Lord who is unfailing love and full redemption. Make it a personal statement of faith. Believe that, whatever area of your life needs redemption, God is willing and able to be the redeemer: of your soul from sin, of your mistakes, failures, and missed opportunities, of your time squandered in selfish pursuits, of your neglect of worship. God's word says His plans for you are for good, to give you hope and a future. Is that not a universal desire?

Even if our comings and goings are not specifically planned around a spiritual pilgrimage, let us lift our eyes and hearts upward. The Maker of heaven and earth is our help and protective watchman. Let us sing a song that exalts the Lord and expresses our hope and trust in His grace and goodness. He is worthy of worship! Great is His Faithfulness!

THANK GOD: Psalm 126:3,5-6 ▪ Psalm 128:1 ▪ Lamentations 3:22-23
TRUST GOD: Psalm 121:1-2,8 ▪ Jeremiah 29:11 ▪ Ephesians 5:15,19-20

Thank God:

Psalm 126:3, 5-6
The Lord has done great things for us, and we are filled with joy.

Those who sow with tears will reap with songs of joy. Those who go out weeping, carrying seed to sow, will return with songs of joy, carrying sheaves with them.

Psalm 128:1
Blessed are all who fear the Lord, who walk in obedience to him.

Lamentations 3:22-23
Because of the Lord's great love we are not consumed, for his compassions never fail. They are new every morning; great is your faithfulness.

Trust God:

Psalm 121:1-2, 8
I lift up my eyes to the mountains—where does my help come from? My help comes from the Lord, the Maker of heaven and earth.

...the Lord will watch over your coming and going both now and forevermore.

Jeremiah 29:11
For I know the plans I have for you," declares the Lord, "plans to prosper you and not to harm you, plans to give you hope and a future."

Ephesians 5:15, 19-20
Be very careful, then, how you live—not as unwise but as wise...

...speaking to one another with psalms, hymns, and songs from the Spirit. Sing and make music from your heart to the Lord, always giving thanks to God the Father for everything, in the name of our Lord Jesus Christ.

For my thoughts are not your thoughts, neither are your ways my ways, declares the Lord.

Isaiah 55: 8

A change of perspective is always a catalyst for new understanding. When problems baffle and buffalo our minds, the "Why me?", "Why now?", "What if?" mentality sets in. Yet one of the most powerful tools in God's storehouse of character-builders and game-changers is a shift in perspective! Maybe your unexpected setback is an opportunity to trust God more, to walk closer to Him, or to discover His better plan. Your situation could become an example to a watching world that God IS a stronghold in the day of trouble. When seeking God's thoughts and His higher ways, a new perspective can affect our priorities and often changes our viewpoint....using the lemons of life to make lemonade!

One day a friend confided in me that she was dreading her high school daughter's departure for college, seeing it as a personal loss even to the point of grief. But late in the Spring of her senior year, the daughter faced a potentially serious medical problem. As the testing continued, my friend's dread shifted from separation fears to fervent prayers that her daughter would be able to go to college! What a change of perspective! What joy when God answered that mother's prayer!

Seek God's perspective on your anxiety, fear, or dread. One pastor put it this way: The Israelites, petrified of giant Goliath, saw the young David with a slingshot as a helpless, hopeless match against the enemy. But courageous David only saw Goliath as so big he could not miss! *

THANK GOD: Isaiah 42:16 ▪ Nahum 1:7 ▪ Isaiah 55:11-12a
TRUST GOD: I Samuel 17:4,45 ▪ II Chronicles 20:6,12 ▪ James 1:4-5

* Charles R. Swindoll, <u>Killing Giants, Pulling Thorns</u>, 1978.

Thank God:

Isaiah 42:16
I will lead the blind by ways they have not known, along unfamiliar paths I will guide them; I will turn the darkness into light before them and make the rough places smooth. These are the things I will do; I will not forsake them.

Nahum 1:7
The Lord is good, a refuge in times of trouble. He cares for those who trust in him...

Isaiah 55:11-12a
...so is my word that goes out from my mouth: It will not return to me empty, but will accomplish what I desire and achieve the purpose for which I sent it. You will go out in joy and be led forth in peace...

Trust God:

I Samuel 17:4, 45
A champion named Goliath, who was from Gath, came out of the Philistine camp. His height was six cubits and a span.

David said to the Philistine, "You come against me with sword and spear and javelin, but I come against you in the name of the Lord Almighty, the God of the armies of Israel, whom you have defied."

II Chronicles 20:6, 12
Lord, the God of our ancestors, are you not the God who is in heaven? You rule over all the kingdoms of the nations. Power and might are in your hand, and no one can withstand you.

Our God, will you not judge them? For we have no power to face this vast army that is attacking us. We do not know what to do, but our eyes are on you.

James 1:4-5
Let perseverance finish its work so that you may be mature and complete, not lacking anything. If any of you lacks wisdom, you should ask God, who gives generously to all without finding fault, and it will be given to you.

Remember the wonders He has done....

I Chronicles 16:12

....great and awesome wonders....

Deuteronomy 10:21

A record of God's faithfulness is a treasure-trove of hope and encouragement. Journal the ways God has answered prayers, provided for needs, guided decisions, brought opportunity for reconciliation, sustained the sick and the weary with strength and healing. Today's hope often depends on our recollection of past wonders....victories God has orchestrated for us over years of trusting and relying on His character, learning from Scriptures and personal experience. Jesus' calming of the storm while in a boat with the disciples becomes the basis for asking the Lord to come into my storm with His calming and His peace. Whether it be a life-crisis storm or vicious weather storm, God's presence and power can see us through.

Judah's King Hezekiah received threatening letters from the king of Assyria, a cruel arch-enemy whose specialty in war was psychological terror. After reading the doomsday letter, the king went to the Temple and spread it out before the Lord, beseeching Him to see and hear the enemy's intimidations and threats. Admitting his country was no match for Assyria, Hezekiah invoked God's deliverance so that all kingdoms on earth would know He alone was God. Try spreading out a troubling paper before the Lord, pleading for his mercy, guidance, and victory over fear. A lawsuit, a divorce paper, a failing report card, a physician's devastating report....spread them out as you humbly seek God's face and will, recalling past wonders from His hidden hand.

THANK GOD: Luke 8:22-25 ▪ II Kings 19:14-19 ▪ Psalm 9:1
TRUST GOD: Psalm 33:20-22 ▪ Psalm 105:4-5 ▪ Deuteronomy 10:21

Thank God:

Luke 8:22-25
One day Jesus said to his disciples, "Let us go over to the other side of the lake." So they got into a boat and set out. As they sailed, he fell asleep. A squall came down on the lake, so that the boat was being swamped, and they were in great danger. The disciples went and woke him, saying, "Master, Master, we're going to drown!" He got up and rebuked the wind and the raging waters; the storm subsided, and all was calm....They asked one another, "Who is this? He commands even the winds and the water, and they obey him."

II Kings 19:14-19
Hezekiah received the letter from the messengers and read it. Then he went up to the temple of the Lord and spread it out before the Lord. And Hezekiah prayed to the Lord: "Lord, the God of Israel, enthroned between the cherubim, you alone are God over all the kingdoms of the earth. You have made heaven and earth. Give ear, Lord, and hear; open your eyes, Lord, and see; listen to the words Sennacherib has sent to ridicule the living God....."Now, Lord our God, deliver us from his hand, so that all the kingdoms of the earth may know that you alone, Lord, are God."

Psalm 9:1
I will give thanks to you, Lord, with all my heart; I will tell of all your wonderful deeds.

Trust God:

Psalm 33:20-22
We wait in hope for the Lord; he is our help and our shield. In him our hearts rejoice, for we trust in his holy name. May your unfailing love be with us, Lord, even as we put our hope in you.

Psalm 105:4-5
Look to the Lord and his strength; seek his face always. Remember the wonders he has done, his miracles, and the judgments he pronounced...

Deuteronomy 10:21
He is the one you praise; he is your God, who performed for you those great and awesome wonders you saw with your own eyes.

He who dwells in the shelter of the Most High
will rest in the shadow of the Almighty.
He is my refuge and my fortress.

Psalm 91:1, 2

In the season of my life when care-giving was the focus of every day, my Bible would automatically open to Isaiah 40 as strength for weariness and power for weakness were daily prayers for loved ones as well as myself. But in the year 2020, security and protection from an unseen enemy became the cry of all hearts. Challenged to trust God's words in Psalm 91, I determined to read and pray the Psalm every day for ninety-one days as we faced a worldwide pandemic. Trusting God's words began to assure my heart and mind. The ninety-one days became a year. Now my Bible opens to Psalm 91....as I seek to dwell and rest securely in a secret place, the shelter of the Most High, Almighty God.

Verses of Psalm 91 cover fears, harms, and hurts that can befall us whatever the year....deadly pestilence, plagues, snares, terrors of night, enemy arrows, mortal dangers, threats, disasters, or destruction. No wonder we tremble from insecurity. But Almighty God is there with us....full of assurances: Under His wing, we find refuge. His faithfulness is our shield. (4) His angels can lift us up over rocky patches. (11-12) We can tread upon and trample mortal attackers. (13) Then, as if all these hopeful reassurances were not enough, the Most High promises His rescue and protection for those who love Him and acknowledge His name. (14) He answers our calls, delivers us from troubles, and satisfies us with prolonged life and His salvation. For ultimate security, trust our Sovereign Savior, who now makes us a dwelling place for His Spirit!

THANK GOD: Isaiah 40:29 ▪ Psalm 91:4 ▪ Psalm 124:7-8
TRUST GOD: Psalm 5:11 ▪ Psalm 34:7 ▪ Ephesians 2:21-22

Thank God:

Isaiah 40:29
He gives strength to the weary and increases the power of the weak.

Psalm 91:4
He will cover you with his feathers, and under his wings you will find refuge; his faithfulness will be your shield and rampart.

Psalm 124:7-8
We have escaped like a bird from the fowler's snare; the snare has been broken, and we have escaped. Our help is in the name of the Lord, the Maker of heaven and earth.

Trust God:

Psalm 5:11
But let all who take refuge in you be glad; let them ever sing for joy. Spread your protection over them, that those who love your name may rejoice in you.

Psalm 34:7
The angel of the Lord encamps around those who fear him, and he delivers them.

Ephesians 2:21-22
In him the whole building is joined together and rises to become a holy temple in the Lord. And in him you too are being built together to become a dwelling in which God lives by his Spirit.

O you of little faith…. do not worry.

Matthew 6:30-31

You of little faith, why are you so afraid?

Matthew 8:26

You of little faith….why did you doubt?

Matthew 14:31

Jesus gave the "little faith" challenge to a large crowd on the side of a mountain, to His own disciples, and to his friend, Peter. Perhaps He is giving it to you today. Does worry, fear, or doubt describe you in the faith category? Jesus gently encourages us toward a growing faith. He compares the kingdom of God to a mustard seed, the smallest seed planted in a garden, growing to become as large as a tree. Our smallest seed of faith can one day bear fruit if it is watered with Jesus' living water and cared for by the Master gardener.

The disciples returned from a mission complaining to Jesus that they could not do what He sent them to do….heal the sick. Jesus said they had "so little faith" and suggested to them a mustard seed faith, as if that would be a giant step for them that day. But we know the rest of their story. After Jesus' resurrection, ascension and the gift of the Holy Spirit, Peter and John healed the crippled beggar at the Temple gate in the name of Jesus Christ. The disciples' "so little faith" grew and bore fruit for His kingdom. *Without faith, it is impossible to please God.* But with faith, Jesus says nothing shall be impossible. Let us ask the God of all possibilities for that mustard seed faith that grows to become both a fruit-bearer and a mountain-mover!

THANK GOD: I Timothy 1:12 ▪ Acts 3:6-8 ▪ Ephesians 2:8-9
TRUST GOD: Matthew 17:20-21 ▪ I Corinthians 2:4-5 ▪ Hebrews 11:6

Thank God:

I Timothy 1:12
I thank Christ Jesus our Lord, who has given me strength, that he considered me trustworthy, appointing me to his service.

Acts 3:6-8
Then Peter said, "Silver or gold I do not have, but what I do have I give you. In the name of Jesus Christ of Nazareth, walk." Taking him by the right hand, he helped him up, and instantly the man's feet and ankles became strong. He jumped to his feet and began to walk. Then he went with them into the temple courts, walking and jumping, and praising God.

Ephesians 2:8-9
For it is by grace you have been saved, through faith—and this is not from yourselves, it is the gift of God—not by works, so that no one can boast.

Trust God:

Matthew 17:20-21
He replied, "Because you have so little faith. Truly I tell you, if you have faith as small as a mustard seed, you can say to this mountain, 'Move from here to there,' and it will move. Nothing will be impossible for you."

I Corinthians 2:4-5
My message and my preaching were not with wise and persuasive words, but with a demonstration of the Spirit's power, so that your faith might not rest on human wisdom, but on God's power.

Hebrews 11:6
And without faith it is impossible to please God, because anyone who comes to him must believe that he exists and that he rewards those who earnestly seek him.

Whoever watches the wind will not plant;
Whoever looks at the clouds will not reap.

Ecclesiastes 11:4

Heavenly Father, I find myself in the "paralysis of analysis" syndrome today. "Maybe...? What if...? If only..." These confusing thoughts are daunting my efforts to make needed decisions. Your wisdom and motivation are necessary to keep moving forward. Watching and looking only at the winds, the clouds, or my own limitations does not encourage positive decision-making or spiritual planting and reaping. My dilemma brings me prayerfully to your throne of grace, asking boldly for your comfort, confidence, and guidance in weighing and making good decisions....desiring always to reflect your best for all involved.

Family relationships, friendships, and professional considerations are invariably part any decision process; so, please, Lord, would you build in me courage and compassion? May your mind be in me, replacing petty imaginations, personal preferences or false hopes with your truth and wisdom. Thank you for hearing this prayer for clarity in my thinking. In Jesus' name, Amen.

Following my prayer for decision-making, I experienced the truth of two Scriptures describing gifts from the Lord. First, the *love* of Christ *that surpasses knowledge* filled my heart as I trusted Him to hear my call. Then, *the _peace_ of God that transcends all understanding* flooded my heart and mind. Thanks be to God for these gifts....and His answers for comfort, courage, compassion, confidence, and guidance!

THANK GOD: Psalm 91:15 ▪ Ephesians 3:19 ▪ Philippians 2:13, 4:7
TRUST GOD: Psalm 145:17-18 ▪ Isaiah 26:3 ▪ Jeremiah 33:3

Thank God:

Psalm 91:15
He will call on me, and I will answer him; I will be with him in trouble, I will deliver him and honor him.

Ephesians 3:19
...and to know this love that surpasses knowledge—that you may be filled to the measure of all the fullness of God.

Philippians 2:13, 4:7
...for it is God who works in you to will and to act in order to fulfill his good purpose.

And the peace of God, which transcends all understanding, will guard your hearts and your minds in Christ Jesus.

Trust God:

Psalm 145:17-18
The Lord is righteous in all his ways and faithful in all he does. The Lord is near to all who call on him, to all who call on him in truth.

Isaiah 26:3
You will keep in perfect peace those whose minds are steadfast, because they trust in you.

Jeremiah 33:3
Call to me and I will answer you and tell you great and unsearchable things you do not know.

Does not the potter have the right
to make out of the
same lump of clay some pottery
for noble purposes
and some for common use?

Romans 9:21

Molded by the hands of a master potter sounds idyllic, until we consider the nature of clay....easily chipped or broken. Though you may have a will of iron and nerves of steel, we are all vulnerable to brokenness! Perhaps you are sidelined, broken right now....wondering if God hears your prayers, or if He could ever use you for any common good, let alone for a noble purpose?

A life-changing promise from Romans 8:28 transforms our perspective: *in all things God works for the good of those who love Him.* "All things" include the cracks or chips in our earthly bodies. The key is our love for God who first loved us, sent His Son as our Redeemer, and calls us to believe in Him. We can ask Jesus to remold us to serve Him in spite of our brokenness.

A story is told of a poor peasant woman who daily would shoulder two large clay pots and trek to a river to retrieve life-giving water. One day an observer laughingly pointed out that one of the pots was cracked, dripping and dribbling water as she walked home. He called her efforts stupid. Calmly replying she was aware of the water loss, she then called attention to a little row of flowers flourishing along her path. "I planted some seeds along this walkway, and every day my cracked clay pot waters them. The blooms bring color, fragrance, and pleasure to my home, and others welcome them as a gift."

Who but God could use a cracked clay pot for a noble purpose? If God has allowed you to be cracked or broken, be not discouraged. Trust Him to use your brokenness to sprinkle His living water on seeds of hope He has planted in hearts along your path!

THANK GOD: Psalm 28:7 ▪ John 4:10 ▪ Romans 8:28-29
TRUST GOD: Proverbs 3:5-6 ▪ Isaiah 41:10 ▪ II Corinthians 4:7,16

Thank God:

Psalm 28:7
The Lord is my strength and my shield; my heart trusts in him, and he helps me. My heart leaps for joy, and with my song I praise him.

John 4:10
Jesus answered her, "If you knew the gift of God and who it is that asks you for a drink, you would have asked him and he would have given you living water."

Romans 8:28-29
And we know that in all things God works for the good of those who love him, who have been called according to his purpose. For those God foreknew he also predestined to be conformed to the image of his Son, that he might be the firstborn among many brothers and sisters.

Trust God:

Proverbs 3:5-6
Trust in the Lord with all your heart and lean not on your own understanding; in all your ways acknowledge him and he will make your paths straight.

Isaiah 41:10
So do not fear, for I am with you; do not be dismayed, for I am your God. I will strengthen you and help you; I will uphold you with my righteous right hand.

II Corinthians 4:7, 16
But we have this treasure in jars of clay to show that this all-surpassing power is from God and not from us. Therefore we do not lose heart. Though outwardly we are wasting away, yet inwardly we are being renewed day by day.

Call on me, and I will answer
you and show you great
and unsearchable things which
you do not know.

Jeremiah 33:3

Few in this age of digital technology will remember when phone numbers began with the first two letters of a word, followed by five digits. (e.g. GLendale 6-3534) Memorizing others' numbers became important! You remembered the word, then the number sequence. One day I was asked if I knew God's phone number? Smiling, I admitted that though I knew and loved God, I did not know His phone number. What I learned in that moment became a life-changer for me. Technology has now advanced dramatically, but I still know one number and have used it daily for decades: JEremiah 33:3 or JE 33:3, as found in the book of Jeremiah, chapter 33, verse 3: a lifetime invitation to call Almighty God.

God encourages us to call Him, so He can show and tell us great things beyond our current experience or understanding. Do not fear that you are being presumptive with God or the Scriptures. Other verses instruct us to do the same thing… Psalm 145:18: "The Lord is near to all who call upon him, to all who call on him in truth." Romans 10:12 reminds us, "For there is no difference between Jew and Gentile—the same Lord is Lord of all and richly blesses all who call on him…."

Are you or a loved one stuck somewhere, seemingly out of options or resources? Has weakness overtaken the strength you once had? Humble yourself. Seek help and hope from the God who created you, redeems you, and can guide you. Make the call: JE 33:3. Tell God in prayer what is on your heart. Listen for His voice, look for His care and guidance, and learn about His faithfulness when you call on Him.

THANK GOD: Psalm 105:1-2 ▪ Jeremiah 32:17 ▪ Ephesians 3:20-21
TRUST GOD: Psalm 34:4 ▪ Psalm 145:17-18 ▪ Isaiah 55:6

Thank God:

Psalm 105:1-2
Give praise to the Lord, proclaim his name; make known among the nations what he has done. Sing to him, sing praise to him; tell of all his wonderful acts.

Jeremiah 32:17
Ah, Sovereign Lord, you have made the heavens and the earth by your great power and outstretched arm. Nothing is too hard for you.

Ephesians 3:20-21
Now to him who is able to do immeasurably more than all we ask or imagine, according to his power that is at work within us, to him be glory in the church and in Christ Jesus throughout all generations, for ever and ever! Amen.

Trust God:

Psalm 34:4
I sought the Lord, and he answered me; he delivered me from all my fears.

Psalm 145:17-18
The Lord is righteous in all his ways and faithful in all he does. The Lord is near to all who call on him, to all who call on him in truth.

Isaiah 55:6
Seek the Lord while he may be found; call on him while he is near.

Jesus said,, "I am the resurrection and the life.....
Whoever lives and believes in me will never die."

John: 11:25-26

John's Gospel reveals remarkable claims Jesus makes about Himself. The "I am" titles summarize the multiple ministry facets of His life. *I am the bread of life; I am the light of the world; I am the good shepherd; I am the way, the truth, and the life.* The repeated "I am" descriptions harken us back to the Old Testament book of Exodus when God called Moses from a burning bush to lead the Hebrew nation out of Egyptian bondage. Moses was hesitant to heed the call. He asked God, who spoke to him in such a dramatic way, to tell him His name. God's answer to Moses: "*I am who I am.* Tell them 'I am' has sent you." As God's Son, Jesus' self-identifying names begin with God's name, "I am".

The "I am" name that most comforts grieving hearts is one Jesus revealed to His friends, Mary and Martha, after Lazarus, their brother, had died and was buried. Jesus wanted all of His followers to know He had power over death, our most feared enemy. *I am the resurrection and the life,* He told the grieving sisters. Then Jesus gave a miraculous demonstration of His claim in the presence of many mourners, as He called Lazarus forth from death to life. Who could doubt His words at that moment? Before long, Jesus Himself would be crucified, dead, buried, then resurrected....personal proof of God's power over death. Seekers at His tomb were told by the angels, "He is risen, just as He said." Jesus is the resurrection and the life for all who live and believe in Him....death has lost its sting! Hallelujah!!

THANK GOD: Exodus 3:13-14 ▪ Matthew 28:5-7 ▪ Luke 24:6
TRUST GOD: John 6:48,51; 8:12; 10:11; 14:6 ▪ I Corinthians 15:55-56

Thank God:

Exodus 3:13-14
Moses said to God, "Suppose I go to the Israelites and say to them, 'The God of your fathers has sent me to you,' and they ask me, 'What is his name?' Then what shall I tell them?" God said to Moses, "I am who I am. This is what you are to say to the Israelites: 'I am has sent me to you.'"

Matthew 28:5-7
The angel said to the women, "Do not be afraid, for I know that you are looking for Jesus, who was crucified. He is not here; he has risen, just as he said. Come and see the place where he lay. Then go quickly and tell his disciples: 'He has risen from the dead and is going ahead of you into Galilee. There you will see him.' Now I have told you."

Luke 24:6
He is not here; he has risen! Remember how he told you, while he was still with you in Galilee...

Trust God:

John 6:48, 51; 8:12; 10:11; 14:6
I am the bread of life....I am the living bread that came down from heaven. Whoever eats this bread will live forever. This bread is my flesh, which I will give for the life of the world.

When Jesus spoke again to the people, he said, "I am the light of the world. Whoever follows me will never walk in darkness, but will have the light of life."

I am the good shepherd. The good shepherd lays down his life for the sheep.

Jesus answered, "I am the way and the truth and the life. No one comes to the Father except through me."

I Corinthians 15:55-56
"Where, O death, is your victory? Where, O death, is your sting?" The sting of death is sin, and the power of sin is the law.

*For our light and momentary troubles are
achieving for us an eternal glory that far
outweighs them all.*

II Corinthians 4:17

If you keep track of news in print or media, you know that human suffering dominates the headlines. Whether it is murder or kidnapping, casualties of war or human error, violent weather or destructive storms, fatal illness or complex health problems, abuse or addiction, the list is endless. No one has a lifetime exemption. Suffering is a part of this fallen world's everyday profile. But God in His powerful goodness offers a contrasting consolation to those who are suffering. By keeping our eyes on unseen, eternal things instead of visible, temporal troubles, we can come to see the pain of suffering in a different light.

Suffering is a simplifier. In the face of pain or personal trauma, few things on a to-do list matter; forget about multi-tasking or productive concentration. Coping becomes our focus. Suffering is also an equalizer. We begin to identify with others who are suffering and find a new empathy for them....even if they were formerly opponents or enemies. Suffering can be a bonding agent across age, rank, education, or economic lines, like the loyal "band of brothers" in wartime, portrayed in literary works old and new. For brothers and sisters in Christ, suffering is a unifier, since God sent His Son to suffer pain and death to bring us into an eternal union with Himself. Jesus knows us; He knows our sufferings; He knows how to redeem and restore us. May we fit a grid of faith over our present sufferings, declaring God's power to use them triumphantly for our good and His glory.

THANK GOD: II Corinthians 4:7 ▪ Hebrews 2:9,18 ▪ I Peter 4:12
TRUST GOD: Psalm 130:5,7 ▪ Romans 5:3-5 ▪ I Peter 5:10

Thank God:

II Corinthians 4:
But we have this treasure in jars of clay to show that this all-surpassing power is from God and not from us.

Hebrews 2:9, 18
But we see Jesus, who was made a little lower than the angels, now crowned with glory and honor because he suffered death, so that by the grace of God he might taste death for everyone.

Because he himself suffered when he was tempted, he is able to help those who are being tempted.

I Peter 4:12
For the eyes of the Lord are on the righteous and his ears are attentive to their prayer, but the face of the Lord is against those who do evil.

Trust God:

Psalm 130:5, 7
I wait for the Lord, my soul waits, and in his word I put my hope.

O Israel, put your hope in the Lord, for with the Lord is unfailing love and with him is full redemption.

Romans 5:3-5
...but we also rejoice in our sufferings, because we know that suffering produces perseverance; perseverance, character; and character, hope. And hope does not disappoint us, because God has poured out his love into our hearts by the Holy Spirit, whom he has given us.

I Peter 5:10
And the God of all grace who called you to his eternal glory in Christ, after you have suffered a little while, will himself restore you and make you strong, firm and steadfast.

*....the God who gives life to the
dead and calls things
that are not as though they were.*

Romans 4:17

Heavenly Father, bring renewal to lifeless relationships in our lives. Resurrect love from ashes of bitterness, resentment, disappointment. Let harmony replace discord and appreciation replace ingratitude. Refresh our hearts with thankfulness for your grace, that your kindness may lead to repentance. Change us, so that forgiveness and gratitude become hall-marks of our relationships: in family, friends, work. Amen.

God has the power and will to answer such a prayer for change in personal behavior and heart attitude. Calling a person to become some-one or something they are not is a specialty of His grace! Whether in families, work settings, or everyday life, we have amazing examples of God's call to His own to become something they were not.

Abraham was called a father of nations before he ever had a son. Moses was called a deliverer in spite of his hesitancy and protests.

Amos was called to prophesy God's judgments though he was a farmer. Peter was called a rock despite denying Jesus. Paul was God's missionary to the Gentiles though he had persecuted and sought to kill Christians. What is God calling you to be, in spite of your limitations or situation? Dr. Howard Hendricks made this observation: "Your career is what you are paid to do. Your calling is what you were made to do." God calls things that are not as though they were. Let His life-giving goodness and power transform you in your family, in your work, or in whatever He is calling you to be which you are not....yet!!

THANK GOD: Ephesians 2:4-5,10 ▪ Romans 2:4 ▪ I Timothy 1:12-14
TRUST GOD: Romans 4:18,20 ▪ Ephesians 4:32 ▪ Colossians 3:13

Thank God:

Ephesians 2:4-5, 10
But because of his great love for us, God, who is rich in mercy, made us alive with Christ even when we were dead in transgressions—it is by grace you have been saved.

For we are God's handiwork, created in Christ Jesus to do good works, which God prepared in advance for us to do.

Romans 2:4
Or do you show contempt for the riches of his kindness, forbearance and patience, not realizing that God's kindness is intended to lead you to repentance?

I Timothy 1:12-14
I thank Christ Jesus our Lord, who has given me strength, that he considered me trustworthy, appointing me to his service. Even though I was once a blasphemer and a persecutor and a violent man, I was shown mercy because I acted in ignorance and unbelief. The grace of our Lord was poured out on me abundantly, along with the faith and love that are in Christ Jesus.

Trust God:

Romans 4:18, 20
Against all hope, Abraham in hope believed and so became the father of many nations, just as it had been said to him, "So shall your offspring be."

Yet he did not waver through unbelief regarding the promise of God, but was strengthened in his faith and gave glory to God...

Ephesians 4:32
Be kind and compassionate to one another, forgiving each other, just as in Christ God forgave you.

Colossians 3:13
Bear with each other and forgive one another if any of you has a grievance against someone. Forgive as the Lord forgave you.

Look to the Lord and his strength, seek his face
always. Remember the wonders he has done.....

I Chronicles 16:11-12

"His strength is perfect when our strength is gone...." Those song lyrics from Steven Curtis Chapman remind us to look to the Lord, asking for His strength when ours is being sapped. * Crisis, illness, fatigue, combat, or caregiving wear us down till a shred of a thread is all the strength we have left. In the face of fleeting strength, always seek the Lord. He knows you and how desperate the situation is. Scripture tells us those who hope and trust in Jesus will never be ashamed. Take God at His word....look, seek, and then do what might seem obvious, but could be difficult for some: Remember the wonders the Lord has done.

Re-energize by recalling wonders, miracles only God could do. Remember God's glorious creation....a fiery sunrise, a glowing sunset, a majestic mountain setting, a roaring waterfall. Has a miracle of God's split-second timing spared your life or saved you from unwise actions? Has He brought across your path a person whose wisdom you needed right then? God uses everyday folk from everyday life, from the Scriptures, even from the nightly news to model miraculous, creative ways He can strengthen us to stay the course, to hang on one minute more, to resume a dread duty with new resolve. Chapman's song lyrics continue, "Raised in His power the weak become strong," declaring the truth that the One whose power raised Jesus from the dead can raise us to new strength. So look to the Lord. Seek His face, remembering His wonders. Then with His strength, press on, trusting and praising Him!

THANK GOD: Psalm 28:7-8 ▪ II Corinthians 12:9 ▪ Ephesians 3:14-16
TRUST GOD: Psalm 31:1,24 ▪ Isaiah 41:10 ▪ Philippians 4:13

* Steven Curtis Chapman, "His Strength Is Perfect", <u>Real Life Conversations</u>, Sparrow Records, 1988.

Thank God:

Psalm 28:7-8
The Lord is my strength and my shield; my heart trusts in him, and he helps me. My heart leaps for joy, and with my song I praise him. The Lord is the strength of his people, a fortress of salvation for his anointed one.

II Corinthians 12:9
But he said to me, "My grace is sufficient for you, for my power is made perfect in weakness." Therefore I will boast all the more gladly about my weaknesses, so that Christ's power may rest on me.

Ephesians 3:14-16
For this reason I kneel before the Father, from whom every family in heaven and on earth derives its name. I pray that out of his glorious riches he may strengthen you with power through his Spirit in your inner being...

Trust God:

Psalm 31:1, 24
In you, Lord, I have taken refuge; let me never be put to shame; deliver me in your righteousness.

Be strong and take heart, all you who hope in the Lord.

Isaiah 41:10
So do not fear, for I am with you; do not be dismayed, for I am your God. I will strengthen you and help you; I will uphold you with my righteous right hand.

Philippians 4:13
I can do all this through him who gives me strength.

For you know the grace of our Lord Jesus Christ,
that though he was rich, yet for your sakes
he became poor, so that you through
his poverty might become rich.

II Corinthians 8:9

When hope is in short supply, meditate on God's amazing grace. <u>G</u>od's <u>R</u>iches <u>A</u>t <u>C</u>hrist's <u>E</u>xpense is an often used definition of grace....a <u>saving grace</u>. Jesus came to die for sinners, to bring victory over death and offer life eternal. <u>Saving grace</u> is a gift we do not deserve and could never earn. Thank Jesus today for dying for you and giving you that victory. Yet God's amazing grace has other blessings here and now for earthly life. Jesus came that we might have a full, abundant life, prior to our eternal one. See if you recognize any of these graces in your life?

Scripture invites believers to come boldly to God's throne of grace to find mercy and receive <u>sufficient grace</u> for our every need. His grace is wise and powerful enough to be perfectly suited to whatever our day may call for. God's <u>surprising grace</u> keeps us on tiptoes about where, when, and how His grace is always greater than we know, enabling us to confront problems, needs, even disappointments. Though seemingly endless trials may challenge us, God's <u>sustaining grace</u> provides endurance, perseverance, and determination to press on. Then when we reach out to others in selfless compassion and generosity, we become a demonstration of God's <u>surpassing grace</u>....favor upon favor. Thank God today for the great grace He grants His people. Trust Him for the particular grace most needed in your life situation today. Ask, and it shall be given to you! Experience the riches of God's amazing grace!

THANK GOD: John 1:7 ▪ II Corinthians 9:8, 11 ▪ II Corinthians 12:9
TRUST GOD: Romans 5:17 ▪ Hebrews 4:16 ▪ I Peter 5:10

Thank God:

John 1:7
He came as a witness to testify concerning that light, so that through him all might believe.

II Corinthians 9:8, 11
And God is able to bless you abundantly, so that in all things at all times, having all that you need, you will abound in every good work.

You will be enriched in every way so that you can be generous on every occasion, and through us your generosity will result in thanksgiving to God.

II Corinthians 12:9
But he said to me, "My grace is sufficient for you, for my power is made perfect in weakness." Therefore I will boast all the more gladly about my weaknesses, so that Christ's power may rest on me.

Trust God:

Romans 5:17
For if, by the trespass of the one man, death reigned through that one man, how much more will those who receive God's abundant provision of grace and of the gift of righteousness reign in life through the one man, Jesus Christ!

Hebrews 4:16
Let us then approach God's throne of grace with confidence, so that we may receive mercy and find grace to help us in our time of need.

I Peter 5:10
And the God of all grace, who called you to his eternal glory in Christ, after you have suffered a little while, will himself restore you and make you strong, firm and steadfast.

For the eyes of the Lord range throughout the earth to strengthen those whose hearts are fully committed to Him.

II Chronicles 16:9

Is it a comfort to you to know that the eyes of the Lord can see everything, everywhere, whether good or evil, finite or spiritual? The thought must make some folks squirm, but for those depending on God alone, what a relief to know His strength is promised to hearts belonging to Him. This truth was actually spoken to a king of Judah as part of a reprimand for seeking a foreign alliance instead of trusting in the Lord when an enemy threatened. Past victories should always be a reminder of God's faithfulness....a "thanks and trust" enhancer when new fears or threats arise.

What makes us forget so quickly how God has rescued or blessed us in the past? The power of fear over rationale and remembrance is the tool of any enemy seeking to undermine faith and trust in God's goodness and His power. If your heart is fully committed to God, by faith in Jesus' atoning death and resurrection, then pray this verse back to your Father in heaven. Thank Him that His eyes see the good and evil on the earth, that He knows you belong to Him. Ask for a strengthening of your heart to trust Him to help you because He has promised it.

God wants us to "be strong and courageous." Think how many times He said just that to Joshua, as if he might forget from one day to the next that the Lord was going to fight for him. Knowing God's word can encourage confidence, no matter the enemy, no matter our fear.

THANK GOD: Proverbs 15:3, 21:3 ▪ I Peter 3:12 ▪ Hebrews 4:13
TRUST GOD: Joshua 1:6-9 ▪ Psalm 32:10 ▪ Psalm 33:18, 20

Thank God:

Proverbs 15:3, 21:3
The eyes of the Lord are everywhere, keeping watch on the wicked and the good.

To do what is right and just is more acceptable to the Lord than sacrifice.

I Peter 3:12
For the eyes of the Lord are on the righteous and his ears are attentive to their prayer, but the face of the Lord is against those who do evil.

Hebrews 4:13
Nothing in all creation is hidden from God's sight. Everything is uncovered and laid bare before the eyes of him to whom we must give account.

Trust God:

Joshua 1:6-9
Be strong and courageous, because you will lead these people to inherit the land I swore to their ancestors to give them. Be strong and very courageous. Be careful to obey all the law my servant Moses gave you; do not turn from it to the right or to the left, that you may be successful wherever you go. Keep this Book of the Law always on your lips; meditate on it day and night, so that you may be careful to do everything written in it. Then you will be prosperous and successful. Have I not commanded you? Be strong and courageous. Do not be afraid; do not be discouraged, for the Lord your God will be with you wherever you go.

Psalm 32:10
Many are the woes of the wicked, but the Lord's unfailing love surrounds the one who trusts in him.

Psalm 33:18, 20
But the eyes of the Lord are on those who fear him, on those whose hope is in his unfailing love...

We wait in hope for the Lord; he is our help and our shield.

*....for it is God who works in you to will and to
act according to his good pleasure.*

Philippians 2:13

God takes pleasure in our obedience. Scripture presents a myriad of opportunities to please Him by taking to heart and obeying His instructions for our thought-life, especially in times of fear or crisis. How obedient am I in specific admonitions from His word? "Do not fret." "Do not be afraid." "Do not let your heart be troubled." "Do not lose heart." "Do not be dismayed." Wait a minute....I am only human! But the wonder of our heavenly Father is that His Holy Spirit provides within us the power <u>not</u> to give into these things. Keeping my focus on Him, I can resist fearfulness, fretting, and loss of hope. Show me, Lord, from your word how and what I should <u>be</u> and <u>do</u> in troubled times.

Be careful. Be calm. (Isaiah 7:4)
Be humble. Be gentle. Be patient. (Ephesians 4:1)
Be strong and courageous.... (Joshua 1:6, 9)
Be joyful in hope, patient in affliction, faithful in prayer. (Romans 12:12)
Set your heart and mind on things above. (Colossians 3:1)
Let the peace of Christ rule in your heart.... (Colossians 3:15)
Let the word of Christ dwell in you richly.... (Colossians 3:16)

Oh, Lord....Put your challenging words to work in me, replacing the time, thoughts, and energy wasted in fear and worry. Make these attributes and actions real in my life as I trust your faithfulness to sustain me in and through hardship, stress, trouble, or life crisis. May it always be my heart's desire to will and do what pleases you. Amen

THANK GOD: Psalm 34:4,19 ▪ Psalm 37:4 ▪ Isaiah 41:10
TRUST GOD: Psalm 56:3-4 ▪ Psalm 91:14-15 ▪ Philippians 4:6-7,19

Thank God:

Psalm 34:4, 19
I sought the Lord, and he answered me; he delivered me from all my fears.

The righteous person may have many troubles, but the Lord delivers him from them all...

Psalm 37:4
Take delight in the Lord, and he will give you the desires of your heart.

Isaiah 41:10
So do not fear, for I am with you; do not be dismayed, for I am your God. I will strengthen you and help you; I will uphold you with my righteous right hand.

Trust God:

Psalm 56:3-4
When I am afraid, I put my trust in you. In God, whose word I praise—in God I trust and am not afraid. What can mere mortals do to me?

Psalm 91:14-15
"Because he loves me," says the Lord, "I will rescue him; I will protect him, for he acknowledges my name. He will call on me, and I will answer him; I will be with him in trouble, I will deliver him and honor him."

Philippians 4:6-7, 19
Do not be anxious about anything, but in every situation, by prayer and petition, with thanksgiving, present your requests to God. And the peace of God, which transcends all understanding, will guard your hearts and your minds in Christ Jesus.

And my God will meet all your needs according to the riches of his glory in Christ Jesus.

For God has not given us the spirit of fear, but of power, and of love, and of a sound mind.

II Timothy 1:7 KJV

You can never predict how knowing God's word will bring hope and courage to a particular moment of your life. A family trip to a world-class amusement park had been idyllic until the moment our two children began begging to go on a new thriller ride, requiring adult accompaniment if they were not a certain height. Never a daring thrill-seeker myself, I began to go into fear-paralysis mode. Strapped in with my daughter awaiting the start signal, she said to me, "Mommie, I can't breathe; you are holding me too tight!" My moment of reckoning had come. My arrow prayer was that God would give me brave thoughts. He did....this verse from II Timothy, learned early in my life as a real scaredy-cat. With my eyes closed, I repeated it over and over. The words sustained me, as we raced, twisted, and spun across the darkness of outer space at breakneck speed....Scripture prayer answered!

This thrill ride was not a life or death moment....yet my fear was real. I often wonder how anyone can prepare to be an astronaut, a soldier, or a first-responder without the Lord and His Word. Fear and her sinister sister, anxiety, are not from God. His gifts are the Holy Spirit's power to overcome and prevail, His unfailing love that holds us tight when we are afraid, and a disciplined, sound mind that can trust and remember God's Word. When next a paralyzing fear presents itself in your life, claim this verse from God....then boldly, bravely take the next step by faith, even if you have to do it a little bit scared.

THANK GOD: Proverbs 9:10 ▪ II Timothy 1:7 NIV ▪ Hebrews 4:16
TRUST GOD: Proverbs 2:6, 3:5-6 ▪ Isaiah 41:10 ▪ Psalm 33:22

Thank God:

Proverbs 9:10
The fear of the Lord is the beginning of wisdom, and knowledge of the Holy One is understanding.

II Timothy 1:7 NIV
For the Spirit God gave us does not make us timid, but gives us power, love and self-discipline.

Hebrews 4:16
Let us then approach God's throne of grace with confidence, so that we may receive mercy and find grace to help us in our time of need.

Trust God:

Proverbs 2:6, 3:5-6
For the Lord gives wisdom; from his mouth come knowledge and understanding.

Trust in the Lord with all your heart and lean not on your own understanding; in all your ways acknowledge him and he will make your paths straight.

Isaiah 41:10
So do not fear, for I am with you; do not be dismayed, for I am your God. I will strengthen you and help you; I will uphold you with my righteous right hand.

Psalm 33:22
May your unfailing love be with us, Lord, even as we put our hope in you.

I will be glad and rejoice in your love, for you saw my affliction and knew the anguish of my soul.

Psalm 31:7

The Lord reigns, let the earth be glad….

Psalm 97:1

"Be glad" is an exhortation often appearing in the Psalms….a response of thankfulness to God for His many blessings. The release of Eleanor Porter's classic children's novel <u>Pollyanna</u> introduced us to the "glad game," finding something to be glad about even when the gift or situation gives no reason for cheer. The story's heroine receives as a gift a set of crutches….an utterly inane gift for the young daughter of a missionary. But instead of complaining resentfully, she says she can "be glad" that she does not need them! Today, a very cheerful, optimistic person is called a "Pollyanna." The name must make God smile, because He wants His children to be glad and thankful, and to say so to Him.

In times of stress or disappointment, we often advise each other to look for a silver lining, or a blessing in disguise. Scripture is clear that because God is able to work all things together for good to those who love Him, we honor His word when we play the "glad game." But those who know and love the Lord do not consider it just a game, but a true reflection of God's goodness and power to change our perspective.

Jesus told those being insulted, persecuted, or unjustly accused, due to their association with Him, to rejoice and be glad because a great heavenly reward awaited them. Even when there is anguish, dismay or disappointment in our souls, the Lord knows when our hearts trust Him enough to "be glad and rejoice" in His unfailing love.

THANK GOD: Psalm 9:1-2 ▪ Psalm 67:4 ▪ Romans 8:28
TRUST GOD: Psalm 5:11 ▪ Matthew 5:11-12 ▪ Psalm 90:14

Thank God:

Psalm 9:1-2
I will give thanks to you, Lord, with all my heart; I will tell of all your wonderful deeds. I will be glad and rejoice in you; I will sing the praises of your name, O Most High.

Psalm 67:4
May the nations be glad and sing for joy, for you rule the peoples with equity and guide the nations of the earth.

Romans 8:28
And we know that in all things God works for the good of those who love him, who have been called according to his purpose.

Trust God:

Psalm 5:11
But let all who take refuge in you be glad; let them ever sing for joy. Spread your protection over them, that those who love your name may rejoice in you.

Matthew 5:11-12
Blessed are you when people insult you, persecute you and falsely say all kinds of evil against you because of me. Rejoice and be glad, because great is your reward in heaven, for in the same way they persecuted the prophets who were before you.

Psalm 90:14
Satisfy us in the morning with your unfailing love, that we may sing for joy and be glad all our days.

Do not be anxious about anything,
but in everything,
by prayer and petition, with thanksgiving,
present your requests to God.

Philippians 4:6

Worry about nothing; pray about everything. If God's word has so instructed us, we can trust Him to enable us, though fleshing it out in times of trial, hardship, or illness is easier said and read than done! Multiple worries become anxieties that move from the mind to the physical body like a paralyzing poison. Has that ever happened to you? Fear is usually the father of anxiety....fear of losing control, fear of failure, fear of losing loved ones or of death itself. The shepherd's Psalm reminds us: *though I walk through the valley of death, I will fear no evil for you are with me; your rod and your staff comfort me.* Jesus is the Good Shepherd who cares for his sheep. Look to the Sovereign Savior for the *peace that passes understanding* and entrust anxieties to Him.

Oh, Lord, please exchange my anxiety for your peace. Show me how to relinquish my worry and fear to you. Like Esther, may I take action with abandonment to You, *"and if I perish, I perish."* Like Charles Spurgeon, may I remember "Our anxiety does not empty tomorrow of its sorrows, but only empties today of its strengths." Stop me from becoming the one of whom Winston Churchill said, "I remember the story of the old man who said on his deathbed that he had had a lot of trouble in his life, most of which had never happened." Keep my mind stayed on You, Lord, that perfect peace may be the result of trusting You. Even in moments of panic or bad news, may I pray to *be anxious for nothing*....thanking Jesus for being the Prince of Peace.

THANK GOD: Esther 4:16 ▪ Psalm 55:22 ▪ Philippians 4:7
TRUST GOD: Psalm 23:4 ▪ Isaiah 26:3 ▪ I Peter 5:7,10

Thank God:

Esther 4:16
"Go, gather together all the Jews who are in Susa, and fast for me. Do not eat or drink for three days, night or day. I and my attendants will fast as you do. When this is done, I will go to the king, even though it is against the law. And if I perish, I perish."

Psalm 55:22
Cast your cares on the Lord and he will sustain you; he will never let the righteous be shaken.

Philippians 4:7
And the peace of God, which transcends all understanding, will guard your hearts and your minds in Christ Jesus.

Trust God:

Psalm 23:4
Even though I walk through the darkest valley, I will fear no evil, for you are with me; your rod and your staff, they comfort me.

Isaiah 26:3
You will keep in perfect peace those whose minds are steadfast, because they trust in you.

I Peter 5:7, 10
Cast all your anxiety on him because he cares for you.

And the God of all grace, who called you to his eternal glory in Christ, after you have suffered a little while, will himself restore you and make you strong, firm and steadfast.

....God disciplines us for our good, that we might share in His holiness.

Hebrews 12:10

HOLY is a word heard and spoken most often about the Lord. The hymn, "Holy, Holy, Holy," juxtaposes humbled, sinful singers with the Lord God Almighty, who is at once merciful; eternal; perfect in love, power, and purity; worthy of worship and praise. Moses' song of victory at the Red Sea praised God Almighty with these words: *O Lord, who is like you—majestic in holiness, awesome in glory, working wonders?* No string of superlatives is adequate to describe Holy God.

Yet God Himself challenges those who belong to Christ *to be holy as I am holy.* Sound impossible? Maybe you fear becoming holy, thinking peers might make fun of you, viewing you with suspicious eyes, judging motives. Yet God instructs His own "to be holy," for *without holiness no one will see God.* Be encouraged by C.S. Lewis: "How little people know who think that holiness is dull. When one meets the real thing, it's irresistible." How then does God let us share in His holiness? Surprisingly, by His discipline! He never promises trial-free living!

Endure hardship as discipline; God is treating you as sons (as daughters). *God disciplines us for our good....to share in His holiness.* Imagine! A hardship you are now enduring is accomplishing an eternal benefit for you, a share of God's holiness. So persevere bravely! Tough situations are teaching tools, not punishment. Hardship is discipline that becomes holiness training. So do not lose heart! Be encouraged and thankful to our Holy God....He wants you to be holy, too.

THANK GOD: Exodus 15:11 ▪ Psalm 29:2 ▪ Isaiah 6:3
TRUST GOD: Leviticus 20:7-8,26 ▪ Hebrews 12:7,14 ▪ I Peter 1:15-16

Thank God:

Exodus 15:11
Who among the gods is like you, Lord? Who is like you—majestic in holiness, awesome in glory, working wonders?

Psalm 29:2
Ascribe to the Lord the glory due his name; worship the Lord in the splendor of his holiness.

Isaiah 6:3
And they were calling to one another: "Holy, holy, holy is the Lord Almighty; the whole earth is full of his glory."

Trust God:

Leviticus 20:7-8, 26
Consecrate yourselves and be holy, because I am the Lord your God. Keep my decrees and follow them. I am the Lord, who makes you holy.

You are to be holy to me because I, the Lord, am holy, and I have set you apart from the nations to be my own.

Hebrews 12:7, 14
Endure hardship as discipline; God is treating you as his children. For what children are not disciplined by their father?

Make every effort to live in peace with everyone and to be holy; without holiness no one will see the Lord.

I Peter 1:15-16
But just as he who called you is holy, so be holy in all you do; for it is written: "Be holy, because I am holy."

....yet I will rejoice in the Lord; I will be joyful in God, my savior.

Habakkuk 3:18

The prophet Habakkuk made this declaration of hope in spite of ominous circumstances he could not fathom. He questions, even doubts, God's justice and judgment in tolerating all the wrongs in the Judean society without bringing judgment on evildoers. When God's answer reveals He is going to do exactly that, using the cruel and merciless Babylonians, then Habakkuk has an even deeper question for God: How could He possibly use the ruthless nation of Babylon to punish the much more righteous Judah? Was not Israel God's chosen nation? Where is God's mercy in all this? How unsearchable are His judgments!

Habakkuk prays again and listens to God: the righteous will live by faith, even when the Lord's Sovereign plans are incomprehensible. With heart pounding, lips quivering, legs trembling, the prophet says he will wait patiently for that day when God will bring His wrath upon the invaders who will force Judah into exile. Habakkuk thinks of all the discouraging losses coming....no buds on fruit trees, no grapes on the vines, failed olive crops, no food, no sheep, no cattle. But he expresses his faith in the Sovereign Lord with the words "Yet I will." In spite of a national disaster, he will rejoice and be joyful in God, his Savior. When facing news of terror, pandemic, scary deprivations, or unexpected loss, let us remember Habakkuk. Reread his prayer, listing our personal dreads. Then may we proclaim ever hopeful, ever confident faith with our own "Yet I will"....Be joyful because we trust a Sovereign Lord, a just God.

THANK GOD: Lamentations 3:22-23 ▪ Hebrews 4:16 ▪ Romans 11:33
TRUST GOD: Psalm 42:5,11 ▪ Habakkuk 3:2,16-19 ▪ Hebrews 11:6

Thank God:

Lamentations 3:22-23
Because of the Lord's great love we are not consumed, for his compassions never fail. They are new every morning; great is your faithfulness.

Hebrews 4:16
Let us then approach God's throne of grace with confidence, so that we may receive mercy and find grace to help us in our time of need.

Romans 11:33
Oh, the depth of the riches of the wisdom and knowledge of God! How unsearchable his judgments, and his paths beyond tracing out!

Trust God:

Psalm 42:5, 11
Why, my soul, are you downcast? Why so disturbed within me? Put your hope in God, for I will yet praise him, my Savior and my God.

Habakkuk 3:2,16-19
Lord, I have heard of your fame; I stand in awe of your deeds, Lord. Repeat them in our day, in our time make them known; in wrath remember mercy.

I heard and my heart pounded, my lips quivered at the sound; decay crept into my bones, and my legs trembled. Yet I will wait patiently for the day of calamity to come on the nation invading us. Though the fig tree does not bud and there are no grapes on the vines, though the olive crop fails and the fields produce no food, though there are no sheep in the pen and no cattle in the stalls, yet I will rejoice in the Lord, I will be joyful in God my Savior. The Sovereign Lord is my strength; he makes my feet like the feet of a deer, he enables me to tread on the heights.

Hebrews 11:6
And without faith it is impossible to please God, because anyone who comes to him must believe that he exists and that he rewards those who earnestly seek him.

God opposes the proud but gives
grace to the humble.

James 4:6

....humility comes before honor.

Proverbs 15:33, 18:12

God puts a high priority on humility, making it a prerequisite for grace and honor. Ever had to admit defeat when a great victory was expected? Do you graciously accept disappointment before you can see any grace or goodness connected to it? Learning humility means banishing pride. Basically, it is believing Jesus when he said, *Apart from me, you can do nothing.* Yet *what is impossible with men is possible with God.* Do you see yourself as a sinner, totally dependent on God...Father, Son, and Holy Spirit....for life, breath, blessings, and a future? These gifts of His grace cannot be earned, deserved, or bought. They must be recognized and received with gratitude by faith in a Sovereign God.

Humility is impossible if pride is blocking thankfulness, and an unforgiving spirit governs attitudes and actions. The humble, thankful heart has a forgiving spirit, acknowledging that Christ's redemption of our sins exhorts us to be forgiving of others. Jesus knows us, loves us, cares for us, calls us by name and has died for us, all before we ever recognize Him as Lord and Savior. He says, *Come to me....learn from me, for I am gentle and humble in heart.* (Matthew 11:28-29) We learn to be humble from His love, mercy, grace, and forgiveness. True humility acknowledges with thankfulness a total dependency on Almighty God, esteeming others as better than ourselves and rejoicing in the honor of receiving the Lord's glorious grace now and forever.

THANK GOD: Psalm 91:15 ▪ Ephesians 2:8-9 ▪ Philippians 2:2-3, 5-8
TRUST GOD: Luke 18:13-14, 27 ▪ John 15:5 ▪ I Peter 5:5-7

Thank God:

Psalm 91:15
He will call on me, and I will answer him; I will be with him in trouble, I will deliver him and honor him.

Ephesians 2:8-9
For it is by grace you have been saved, through faith—and this is not from yourselves, it is the gift of God—not by works, so that no one can boast.

Philippians 2:2-3, 5-8
Do nothing out of selfish ambition or vain conceit. Rather, in humility value others above yourselves.... In your relationships with one another, have the same mindset as Christ Jesus: Who, being in very nature God, did not consider equality with God something to be used to his own advantage; rather, he made himself nothing by taking the very nature of a servant, being made in human likeness. And being found in appearance as a man, he humbled himself by becoming obedient to death—even death on a cross!

Trust God:

Luke 18:13-14
But the tax collector stood at a distance. He would not even look up to heaven, but beat his breast and said, "God, have mercy on me, a sinner." I tell you that this man, rather than the other, went home justified before God. For all those who exalt themselves will be humbled, and those who humble themselves will be exalted.

John 15:5
I am the vine; you are the branches. If you remain in me and I in you, you will bear much fruit; apart from me you can do nothing.

I Peter 5:5-7
In the same way, you who are younger, submit yourselves to your elders. All of you, clothe yourselves with humility toward one another, because, "God opposes the proud but shows favor to the humble." Humble yourselves, therefore, under God's mighty hand, that he may lift you up in due time. Cast all your anxiety on him because he cares for you.

*My soul, wait thou only upon God; for my
expectations are from him.*

Psalm 62:5 KJV

*Find rest, O my Soul, in God alone; my
hope comes from him.*

Psalm 62:5 NIV

Be careful about putting expectations and hopes on anything or anyone except God Himself. Whenever we do, we set ourselves up for disappointment. Human hopes and expectations can intertwine in ways that leads to confusion, displeasure, anger, a judgmental attitude, or even a broken relationship. Our personal hopes often put unrealistic expectations on others....and when they do not respond as hoped, we are let down, even crushed with disappointment. In turn, others' expectations of us build pressure to act or respond in a way that might be impractical or even unwise. Guard against letting personal hopes become definite expectations, unless it is God Himself who has promised it in His Word. Then we can hope expectantly and trust in Him for fulfillment in His timing, not ours.

Our souls find rest as we wait on the Lord. We look to the God of Hope to give us hope and an expectancy about receiving what He has promised. Great is His faithfulness! He already knows our inward thoughts and needs. God knows when our desire is to let Him choose the best remedy, best response, best solution for our difficulties, including distressing upsets in personal relations stemming from unmet expectations. Seek God's best....put your expectations and hopes in His hands. Then wait on the Lord, resting in His wisdom, grace, and timing.

THANK GOD: Psalm 91:1-2 ▪ Psalm 116:7 ▪ Romans 15:13
TRUST GOD: Psalm 28:7 ▪ Psalm 62:1-2,8 ▪ Isaiah 12:2

Thank God:

Psalm 91:1-2
Whoever dwells in the shelter of the Most High will rest in the shadow of the Almighty. I will say of the Lord, "He is my refuge and my fortress, my God, in whom I trust."

Psalm 116:7
Return to your rest, my soul, for the Lord has been good to you.

Romans 15:13
May the God of hope fill you with all joy and peace as you trust in him, so that you may overflow with hope by the power of the Holy Spirit.

Trust God:

Psalm 28:7
The Lord is my strength and my shield; my heart trusts in him, and he helps me. My heart leaps for joy, and with my song I praise him.

Psalm 62:1-2, 8
Truly my soul finds rest in God; my salvation comes from him. Truly he is my rock and my salvation; he is my fortress, I will never be shaken.

Trust in him at all times, you people; pour out your hearts to him, for God is our refuge.

Isaiah 12:2
Surely God is my salvation; I will trust and not be afraid. The Lord, the Lord himself, is my strength and my defense; he has become my salvation.

Let the morning bring me word of your
unfailing love, for I have put my trust in you.

Psalm 143:8

If you have ever had to leave a loved one overnight in the hospital, you know the dread of the long night ahead....anxiety, fear, worry. But God in His grace always has a word of comfort and hope for the heavy heart. On one such night for me, some verses from Psalm 143 gave me words to pray when my mind was having trouble even thinking of how to pray. *O Lord, hear my prayer, listen to my cry for mercy.*[v1] *My Spirit grows faint within me; my heart within me is dismayed.*[v4] *Answer me quickly, O Lord; my spirit fails.*[v7] Speaking the truth to God in prayer about a situation opens a way for us to see we are not alone. God is there, He cares, and He is with us to give comfort. I faced that dark night by ending my prayer with this petition: *Let the morning bring me word of your unfailing love, for I have put my trust in you.* Praying God's word back to Him affirms our trust that we can rest in Him.

Upon awaking the next morning, I could rejoice and thank God that I was able to sleep. Whether your patient's stay is overnight or much longer, ask the Lord for His peace. In times of aloneness during any tumultuous situation, medical emergency or even in a long and scary pandemic, remember to ask for God's comforting mercy. Describe your feelings, and petition Him from His word about your hopes and fears, using the Psalms as a Prayer Book. Then put your trust in God as you rest in peaceful sleep till the morning brings you word of His unfailing love. Great is His faithfulness!

THANK GOD: Psalm 33:20-22 ▪ Psalm 147:11 ▪ Psalm 103:1-2
TRUST GOD: Psalm 6:4 ▪ Psalm 57:1 ▪ Psalm 90:14

Thank God:

Psalm 33:20-22
We wait in hope for the Lord; he is our help and our shield. In him our hearts rejoice, for we trust in his holy name. May your unfailing love be with us, Lord, even as we put our hope in you.

Psalm 147:11
...the Lord delights in those who fear him; who put their hope in his unfailing love.

Psalm 103:1-2
Praise the Lord, my soul; all my inmost being, praise his holy name. Praise the Lord, my soul, and forget not all his benefits...

Trust God:

Psalm 6:4
Turn, Lord, and deliver me; save me because of your unfailing love.

Psalm 57:1
Have mercy on me, my God, have mercy on me, for in you I take refuge. I will take refuge in the shadow of your wings until the disaster has passed.

Psalm 90:14
Satisfy us in the morning with your unfailing love, that we may sing for joy and be glad all our days.

Even to your old age and grey hairs, I am he....
who will sustain you.... I have made you....
will carry you....will rescue you.

Isaiah 46:4

An irony of earthly life is that the young cannot wait to be older, and the ageing long for the days of youth. Thanks be to God for His assurance that just as He was our confidence in our youth, greying heads can also claim the promise of His sustaining power! With ageing, hopes sometimes follow the body's lead....frail and weak, failing sight, difficulty hearing, challenging mobility, feelings of uselessness. Do those descriptions fit you or a loved one? Take heart! God has encouragement for the older years....to revive and renew your hope and trust in Him.

Need stamina or strength? God promises to be your sustainer....and remember that His strength is perfected in weakness (an irony of our Lord). Admit your need and increase dependency on God's supply (Philippians 4:19). He created you and knows exactly how you are best kept strong. Daily read His word in hope and preparation for whatever He knows is ahead of you....a new season of usefulness and service!

Need God's carrying power? God rescues us when we are not able to carry ourselves forward. A modern parable pictures a life journey marked by two sets of footprints proceeding together as companions ....God and one of His own. Suddenly there is only one set of footprints. "Lord, where were you at that moment? Did you leave me alone?" God's reply is "Never....that is when I carried you through a heart-breaking time." Thankfully, our Lord will sustain, carry, and rescue us as we continue to thank and trust Him, no matter our age or stage.

THANK GOD: Psalm 37:25 ▪ Psalm 71:5,17-18 ▪ Jeremiah 29:11
TRUST GOD: Psalm 92:14-15 ▪ Psalm 91:15 ▪ II Thessalonians 2:16

Thank God:

Psalm 37:25
I was young and now I am old, yet I have never seen the righteous forsaken or their children begging bread.

Psalm 71:5, 17-18
For you have been my hope, Sovereign Lord, my confidence since my youth.

Since my youth, God, you have taught me, and to this day I declare your marvelous deeds. Even when I am old and gray, do not forsake me, my God, till I declare your power to the next generation, your mighty acts to all who are to come.

Jeremiah 29:11
For I know the plans I have for you," declares the Lord, "plans to prosper you and not to harm you, plans to give you hope and a future."

Trust God:

Psalm 92:14-15
They will still bear fruit in old age, they will stay fresh and green, proclaiming, "The Lord is upright; he is my Rock, and there is no wickedness in him."

Psalm 91:15
He will call upon me, and I will answer him; I will be with him and honor him. With long life I will satisfy him and show him my salvation.

II Thessalonians 2:16
...our Lord Jesus Christ himself and God our Father, who loved us and by his grace gave us eternal encouragement and good hope...

A cheerful look brings joy to the heart, and good news gives health to the bones.

Proverbs 15:30

Never underestimate the power of your smile! Sound like an advertisement for a dental practice? Surprisingly, a smile could be a heart strengthener. The joy of the Lord was said by Nehemiah to be the source of his strength....so if you are joyful in the Lord, too, He may use your cheerful look to benefit another. How thrilling to think that something as simple as a sparkling smile could mean joy and strength to others' hearts and health! No wonder little Orphan Annie sang, "You are never fully dressed without your smile." Remember that small things done with love can make a big difference!

What's more, the book of Proverbs offers tips about having healthy bones....not treatment recommendations, but life habits we can adopt, like hearing and bearing good news (Bible verses about God's love and grace, a message from family far away, the revelation of a personal victory). Add to good news a fear of the Lord, the shunning of evil, and a use of pleasant words....all contribute nourishment to our bones. But be aware of this warning....*a crushed spirit dries up the bones*! So reach out with loving concern to teenagers and others who are vulnerable to the crushing of their spirits by social media pettiness, meanness, or falsehoods....damaging their spirits (and their bones). Ask God to help you become His agent of joy, hope, and health by heeding His words of wisdom and warning in Proverbs, beginning today!

THANK GOD: Nehemiah 8:10 ▪ Psalm 139:14 ▪ Proverbs 3:7
TRUST GOD: Proverbs 15:13 ▪ Proverbs 16:24 ▪ Proverbs 17:22

Thank God:

Nehemiah 8:10
Nehemiah said, "Go and enjoy choice food and sweet drinks, and send some to those who have nothing prepared. This day is holy to our Lord. Do not grieve, for the joy of the Lord is your strength."

Psalm 139:14
I praise you because I am fearfully and wonderfully made; your works are wonderful, I know that full well.

Proverbs 3:7
Do not be wise in your own eyes; fear the Lord and shun evil.

Trust God:

Proverbs 15:13
A happy heart makes the face cheerful, but heartache crushes the spirit.

Proverbs 16:24
Gracious words are a honeycomb, sweet to the soul and healing to the bones.

Proverbs 17:22
A cheerful heart is good medicine, but a crushed spirit dries up the bones.

He will cover you with His feathers and under His wings you will find refuge.

Psalm 91:4

The poet Emily Dickinson described HOPE in an extraordinary way: "the thing with feathers that perches in the soul...the thing that sings the tune without the words and never stops at all." Hope as a "feathered thing"....how creative! Yet Scriptures do relate rescue and hope with feathers....like a protective mother bird gathering her babies under her wing when danger is present, or a brooding hen protecting her chicks from a predator nearby. Jesus Himself used the analogy.

Ironically, wispy feathers do not appear strong enough to protect anything. But the combination of intricately overlapping feathers and the muscle power of a wing, strong enough for flight, aid the instinct to protect at all costs....a picture of God's power and desire to surround and protect His children. *The Lord is our refuge and strength, a very present help in trouble.* A strong refuge fans the embers of hopefulness.

Following deadly wildfires in Yellowstone National Park, a modern day parable surfaced. Rangers surveying the damage were said to have found a bird on the ground, petrified in ashes. Why had the bird not flown away or perched up higher? As the lifeless bird figure was knocked over, baby birds came scurrying out. The mother bird had instinctively protected them under her wings. She died, but chicks under the cover of her wings lived. Under God's protective wings, your life has been preserved by the death of His Son. He secures your hope for eternal life, and the "feathers" of His faithfulness can protect us in the here and now.

THANK GOD: Psalm 46:1 ▪ Psalm 91:2 ▪ Luke 13:34
TRUST GOD: Psalm 17:8 ▪ Psalm 36:7 ▪ Psalm 57:1

Thank God:

Psalm 46:1
God is our refuge and strength, an ever-present help in trouble.

Psalm 91:2
I will say of the Lord, "He is my refuge and my fortress, my God, in whom I trust."

Luke 13:34
Jerusalem, Jerusalem, you who kill the prophets and stone those sent to you, how often I have longed to gather your children together, as a hen gathers her chicks under her wings, and you were not willing.

Trust God:

Psalm 17:8
Keep me as the apple of your eye; hide me in the shadow of your wings...

Psalm 36:7
How priceless is your unfailing love, O God! People take refuge in the shadow of your wings.

Psalm 57:1
Have mercy on me, my God, have mercy on me, for in you I take refuge. I will take refuge in the shadow of your wings until the disaster has passed.

He performs wonders that cannot be fathomed,
miracles that cannot be counted.

Job 9:10

God is in the business of wonders and miracles of every kind and size. His infinite creativity can arrange a supernatural intervention of dramatic proportions, as well as small, everyday wonders of His grace and timing. We cannot measure God's power and goodness. What is big and what is small, only He can tell. Just thank Him that He knows right where we are and cares about the burdens and desires of our hearts.

When my husband became ill, my heart cried out in prayer to God to make a way for him to survive his cancer. During the two years of his illness, operations, and treatment, countless glimmers of God's grace and goodness comforted and encouraged us. Journal notes reminded me of everyday gifts of the Lord's faithfulness: the support and prayers of friends and family, kindnesses from medical personnel, my sustained good health as a caregiver, effective pain control, the relatively short time he was totally helpless, and strategic, comforting pastoral visits. Yet in the darkness of grief and disappointment that my husband would not be a cancer survivor, it was God's words in Scripture that empowered me not to fear, but to trust my heavenly Father....to cast all my anxieties upon Him, because He cared for me and my loved one.

God's ways are always higher than ours; often they are past finding out. But if you are inching toward hopelessness about a crisis situation in your life, then boldly approach the One whose power can daily perform unfathomable wonders and countless miracles as you trust Him, even when the heart's cry is denied a "yes" answer.

THANK GOD: Isaiah 55:8-9 ▪ Psalm 27:13-14 ▪ Romans 11:33
TRUST GOD: Hebrews 11:5 ▪ Psalm 119:41-42,49 ▪ I Peter 5:7

Thank God:

Isaiah 55:8-9
"For my thoughts are not your thoughts, neither are your ways my ways," declares the Lord. "As the heavens are higher than the earth, so are my ways higher than your ways and my thoughts than your thoughts."

Psalm 27:13-14
I remain confident of this: I will see the goodness of the Lord in the land of the living. Wait for the Lord; be strong and take heart and wait for the Lord.

Romans 11:33
Oh, the depth of the riches of the wisdom and knowledge of God! How unsearchable his judgments, and his paths beyond tracing out!

Trust God:

Hebrews 11:5
By faith Enoch was taken from this life, so that he did not experience death: "He could not be found, because God had taken him away." For before he was taken, he was commended as one who pleased God.

Psalm 119:41-42, 49
May your unfailing love come to me, Lord, your salvation, according to your promise; then I can answer anyone who taunts me, for I trust in your word.

Remember your word to your servant, for you have given me hope.

I Peter 5:7
Cast all your anxiety on him because he cares for you.

As they began to sing and praise, the Lord set ambushes against the men....who were invading Judah.

II Chronicles 20:22

God is always more amazing than we know, especially when we have few options against a strong enemy. Foes come against us many ways....an invading army, an assault of fearful anxiety, a personal crisis resulting from another's wrong choices. The question arises: what am I to do? First, seek God and His word. Recall King Jehoshaphat, crying out in desperation: *We do not know what to do, but our eyes are upon you.* (II Chronicles 20:12) Follow his example: begin to sing and praise the Lord.

Sound too simple? Maybe, but never underestimate the power of singing to the Lord, praising His holy name. The King of Judah, fearful of invading armies, appointed his men to sing and praise the Lord. And as they did, God set ambushes against their multiple enemies, who began to fight among themselves, slaughtering and annihilating each other.... leaving behind more plunder than could be taken away in a day.

In Acts 16, Paul and Silas were praying and singing hymns at midnight in prison after having been beaten, flogged, and shackled. A sudden, violent earthquake shook the prison, opening the doors and loosing their chains. The distraught jailor, fearing all had escaped, came to faith in Christ when Paul shared with him about believing in Jesus.

If you are facing a strong enemy today, focus on God. Sing "Holy, Holy, Holy" and "A Mighty Fortress." Praise God that the battle is His. Then *stand firm and see* what the Lord will do against your enemy.

THANK GOD: I Chronicles 16:29 ▪ II Chronicles 20:23, 29 ▪ Psalm 147:1
TRUST GOD: Psalm 13:5-6 ▪ Psalm 33:1 ▪ Ephesians 5:19-20

Thank God:

I Chronicles 16:29
Ascribe to the Lord the glory due his name; bring an offering and come before him. Worship the Lord in the splendor of his holiness.

II Chronicles 20:20-22, 29
Early in the morning they left for the Desert of Tekoa. As they set out, Jehoshaphat stood and said, "Listen to me, Judah and people of Jerusalem! Have faith in the Lord your God and you will be upheld; have faith in his prophets and you will be successful." After consulting the people, Jehoshaphat appointed men to sing to the Lord and to praise him for the splendor of his holiness as they went out at the head of the army, saying: "Give thanks to the Lord, for his love endures forever." As they began to sing and praise, the Lord set ambushes against the men of Ammon and Moab and Mount Seir who were invading Judah, and they were defeated.

The fear of God came on all the surrounding kingdoms when they heard how the Lord had fought against the enemies of Israel.

Psalm 147:1
Praise the Lord. How good it is to sing praises to our God, how pleasant and fitting to praise him!

Trust God:

Psalm 13:5-6
But I trust in your unfailing love; my heart rejoices in your salvation. I will sing the Lord's praise, for he has been good to me.

Psalm 33:1
Sing joyfully to the Lord, you righteous; it is fitting for the upright to praise him.

Ephesians 5:19-20
…speaking to one another with psalms, hymns, and songs from the Spirit. Sing and make music from your heart to the Lord, always giving thanks to God the Father for everything, in the name of our Lord Jesus Christ.

May your unfailing love rest upon us, O Lord,
even as we put our hope in you.

Psalm 33:22

The God of Hope is our hope, and our hope in Him is not in vain. If you were to be asked today about your hopes, you might have several categories: present day hopes (enough money to pay bills), long-range hopes (education or professional skills), lifetime hopes (living a life that pleases God, with opportunity to serve others in a meaningful way). Our every hope depends somehow on the Lord to become reality.

So how do we hope in the Lord and not in ourselves? Start by not taking matters into our own hands or complaining impatiently or manipulating people or events toward a desired outcome. By realizing God's unfailing love rests upon us, our stress is softened. When we know and fear the Lord, we trustingly put our hope in Him. In keeping with God's holiness and goodness, He has the power to do what is best for His own. Our part is believing He can and will do that for us in terms of our hopes. What is best for us is something He alone knows.

Not only do we put our hope in God, but He Himself is our hope, our best hope. Pray for God's best in your hopes, refusing to think a particular person, acquisition, or event is always the answer. Our minds have trouble leaving everything to God's power and grace, not relying on something or someone else to fulfill hopes for us. Recognize your dependency on the Lord; rest in His unfailing love, even when circumstances seem anything but hopeful. Tell Him every morning: "You are my hope, God of Hope; I wait in hope on you alone."

THANK GOD: Psalm 107:21 ▪ Jeremiah 29:11 ▪ Romans 15:13
TRUST GOD: Psalm 40:5 ▪ Romans 4:20-21 ▪ I Timothy 6:17

Thank God:

Psalm 107:21
Let them give thanks to the Lord for his unfailing love and his wonderful deeds for mankind.

Jeremiah 29:11
"For I know the plans I have for you," declares the Lord, "plans to prosper you and not to harm you, plans to give you hope and a future."

Romans 15:13
May the God of hope fill you with all joy and peace as you trust in him, so that you may overflow with hope by the power of the Holy Spirit.

Trust God:

Psalm 40:5
Many, Lord my God, are the wonders you have done, the things you planned for us. None can compare with you; were I to speak and tell of your deeds, they would be too many to declare.

Romans 4:20-21
Yet he did not waver through unbelief regarding the promise of God, but was strengthened in his faith and gave glory to God, being fully persuaded that God had power to do what he had promised.

I Timothy 6:17
Command those who are rich in this present world not to be arrogant nor to put their hope in wealth, which is so uncertain, but to put their hope in God, who richly provides us with everything for our enjoyment.

The God of all grace, who called
you to his eternal glory in Christ, after you
have suffered a little while, will himself
make you, strong, firm, and steadfast.

I Peter 5:10

A New Year had just dawned. The bright, golden faces of sunflowers beckoned from a flower stand open on New Year's Day. Gratitude for a new start, a clean slate, stirred me to buy a dozen of the stately beauties....one for each month of the new year. My heart longed for a symbolic exchange of the previous year's "Suffering-of-the-month" pattern for a new series called "Joy-of-the-month."

The eye-catching bouquet made me smile, delighting my heart. The blooms varied in some ways, but the twelve together created a beauty en mass that spoke of the blessing of a friendship network offered by those God has placed around us....individually different, but fitting together like a strong safety net, supporting each other with cheerful care and a joy in the Lord, even in the face of trial or trouble.

Lord, let me be like a sunflower this year....a radiant face, a simple but inviting presence, a tough, sturdy center stem not easily broken....resilient against adversity, but fearlessly faithful to stand upright in dependency on You. As the God of all grace, please uphold me in times of suffering as I claim your promise that afterwards you will make me stronger in my faith, firmer in my foundation on your word, and more steadfast in my trust of your goodness! Allow me to be part of an arrangement of friends who can stand together around one another, encouraging each other with words of hope and Christ's eternal glory.

THANK GOD: Isaiah 58:11 ▪ Acts 20:32 ▪ Romans 5:17
TRUST GOD: Psalm 56:3-4 ▪ Psalm 62:5 ▪ Ephesians 4:2

Thank God:

Isaiah 58:11
The Lord will guide you always; he will satisfy your needs in a sun-scorched land and will strengthen your frame. You will be like a well-watered garden, like a spring whose waters never fail.

Acts 20:32
Now I commit you to God and to the word of his grace, which can build you up and give you an inheritance among all those who are sanctified.

Romans 5:17
For if, by the trespass of the one man, death reigned through that one man, how much more will those who receive God's abundant provision of grace and of the gift of righteousness reign in life through the one man, Jesus Christ!

Trust God:

Psalm 56:3-4
When I am afraid, I put my trust in you. In God, whose word I praise—in God I trust and am not afraid. What can mere mortals do to me?

Psalm 62:5
Yes, my soul, find rest in God; my hope comes from him.

Ephesians 4:2
Be completely humble and gentle; be patient, bearing with one another in love.

*Wisdom brightens a man's face and
changes its hard appearance.*

Ecclesiastes 8:1

Have you ever chuckled as you read a verse of Scripture? Beside this verse in my Bible, I wrote, "God's facelift!" Who but God could offer "wisdom" as an Rx for changing a hard appearance to a softer, brighter face? In today's preoccupation with personal appearance, even children notice changes as their parents grow older. A friend shared with me her young daughter's comment as they were looking at the mother's wedding album. With a sincere, straight face the little girl said, "Mommy, I like your face better then." One pastor has wisely observed that technology will never overcome biology. The search for ways to keep a youthful appearance is not new. Spanish Explorer Ponce de Leon hoped to find a Fountain of Youth in his Florida wanderings in 1513. But God's facelift does not require surgery, technology, or travel.

So how does one get the "wisdom" that changes the hard appearance of a face? The Scriptures tell us *the fear of the Lord is the beginning of wisdom*. When faithful Moses came down from Mt. Sinai, he was unaware *his face was radiant because he had spoken with the Lord*. But others noticed. Christ himself is declared to be *the power and the wisdom of God....*that wisdom can be a face changer. Fear the Lord, speak often with Him. Knowledge of His Son is a foundation for wisdom. If you seek a brighter face, ask God today for His wisdom "face-lift" as you gratefully express trust in Jesus Christ as your Savior. Then it will be true that you are among those about whom the Psalmist proclaimed, *Those who look to Him are radiant...!*

THANK GOD: Proverbs 9:10 ▪ James 1:5-6 ▪ Exodus 34:29
TRUST GOD: I Corinthians 1:24 ▪ Psalm 34:5 ▪ Psalm 111:10

Thank God:

Proverbs 9:10
The fear of the Lord is the beginning of wisdom, and knowledge of the Holy One is understanding.

James 1:5-6
If any of you lacks wisdom, you should ask God, who gives generously to all without finding fault, and it will be given to you. But when you ask, you must believe and not doubt, because the one who doubts is like a wave of the sea, blown and tossed by the wind.

Exodus 34:29
When Moses came down from Mount Sinai with the two tablets of the covenant law in his hands, he was not aware that his face was radiant because he had spoken with the Lord.

Trust God:

I Corinthians 1:24
...but to those whom God has called, both Jews and Greeks, [we preach] Christ the power of God and the wisdom of God.

Psalm 34:5
Those who look to him are radiant; their faces are never covered with shame.

Psalm 111:10
The fear of the Lord is the beginning of wisdom; all who follow his precepts have good understanding. To him belongs eternal praise.

See, I have engraved you on the
palms of my hands…..

Isaiah 49:16

Years before computers and the GPS, bush pilots used to write important coordinates on their hands, to review them quickly to maintain a flight pattern. Safety and wellbeing could depend on this writing on the palm of a hand. Isaiah uses a similar, symbolic illustration to picture how important each believer is to the Lord, especially if they feel God has forgotten or forsaken them. When we need His wisdom and guidance, His compassion and reassurance, we can come at once to Him because we, by name, are always "in his grip".

Before the Hebrews entered the promised land, God instructed Moses to build a portable tabernacle, called the Tent of Meeting. God met with His appointed leaders there and gave them a pattern of worship for the nation. Aaron, named by God as the first high priest, got specific instructions for his priestly attire: the outer garment (the ephod) was to be fastened at each shoulder with a stone engraved with the names of the twelve tribes of Israel….six names on either side. Upon entering into God's Holy Place, the high priest brought before the Lord as a memorial these engraved names of His chosen people's identity.

Beloved children of God, picture your name written on the nail-scarred hands of Jesus, your high priest, as He brings you before the presence of His Father. He knows your name, and He has you in His grip. Trust His truth: *I will never leave you or forsake you.* Thank Him for the unfailing love that grips and holds you close in His abiding presence.

THANK GOD: Exodus 28:9-12 ▪ John 10:3,27-29 ▪ Hebrews 7:24-25
TRUST GOD: Joshua 1:5,9 ▪ Isaiah 25:4 ▪ Revelation 3:5

Thank God:

Exodus 28:9-12
Take two onyx stones and engrave on them the names of the sons of Israel in the order of their birth—six names on one stone and the remaining six on the other. Engrave the names of the sons of Israel on the two stones the way a gem cutter engraves a seal....Aaron is to bear the names on his shoulders as a memorial before the Lord.

John 10:3, 27-29
The gatekeeper opens the gate for him, and the sheep listen to his voice. He calls his own sheep by name and leads them out.

My sheep listen to my voice; I know them, and they follow me. I give them eternal life, and they shall never perish; no one will snatch them out of my hand. My Father, who has given them to me, is greater than all; no one can snatch them out of my Father's hand.

Hebrews 7:24-25
...but because Jesus lives forever, he has a permanent priesthood. Therefore he is able to save completely those who come to God through him, because he always lives to intercede for them.

Trust God:

Joshua I:5, 9
No one will be able to stand against you all the days of your life. As I was with Moses, so I will be with you; I will never leave you nor forsake you.

Have I not commanded you? Be strong and courageous. Do not be afraid; do not be discouraged, for the Lord your God will be with you wherever you go.

Isaiah 25:4
You have been a refuge for the poor, a refuge for the needy in their distress, a shelter from the storm and a shade from the heat.

Revelation 3:5
The one who is victorious will, like them, be dressed in white. I will never blot out the name of that person from the book of life, but will acknowledge that name before my Father and his angels.

For I know the plans I have for you....plans to prosper you and not to harm you, plans to give you hope and a future.

Jeremiah 29:11

Exiled in Babylon, far from their homeland, without any elements of normal life or worship, God's chosen people mourned and lamented: "By the rivers of Babylon we sat and wept when we remembered Zion." While their harps hung on poplar trees, their captors tormented them, demanding songs of joy. "Sing us one of the songs of Zion!" Who among exiles ever feels like singing, especially when being goaded and mocked by an enemy? But God sent encouragement in the form of a letter from His prophet Jeremiah, exhorting hope rather than despair, reminding them that God's plans were always for their good, promising a time when Israel would return to their homeland. He even challenged them to be good citizens and to pray for the city of their exile. (Jeremiah 29:7) Imagine that!!

Have you ever felt like an exile? Even in familiar territory, it takes an emotional toll, like the fearful quarantine isolation during a virus pandemic. Maybe you are the only one in your family who is trusting in God. Perhaps you are a lone figure at work refusing to go along with unethical practices or malicious gossip. Are you a single parent wishing you had a different status, hoping for a change? The Lord has plans for you right where you are. Use the self-talk of Psalm 42:5: *Why are you downcast, O my soul? Why so disturbed within me? Put your hope in God, for I shall yet praise him, my Savior and my God.* His plans for you are for good....even if His timing is not yours. Wait with patience, trust His love and goodness, and anticipate a day when your joyful song praises the Lord's rescue plan!

THANK GOD: Job 23:10 ▪ Psalm 62:5-6 ▪ Psalm 92:4
TRUST GOD: Psalm 33:20-22 ▪ Psalm 91:14-15 ▪ Psalm 137:1-3

Thank God:

Job 23:10
But he knows the way that I take; when he has tested me, I will come forth as gold.

Psalm 62:5-6
Yes, my soul, find rest in God; my hope comes from him. Truly he is my rock and my salvation; he is my fortress, I will not be shaken.

Psalm 92:4
For you make me glad by your deeds, Lord; I sing for joy at what your hands have done.

Trust God:

Psalm 33:20-22
We wait in hope for the Lord; he is our help and our shield. In him our hearts rejoice, for we trust in his holy name. May your unfailing love be with us, Lord, even as we put our hope in you.

Psalm 91:14-15
"Because he loves me," says the Lord, "I will rescue him; I will protect him, for he acknowledges my name. He will call on me, and I will answer him; I will be with him in trouble, I will deliver him and honor him."

Psalm 137:1-3
By the rivers of Babylon we sat and wept when we remembered Zion. There on the poplars we hung our harps, for there our captors asked us for songs, our tormentors demanded songs of joy; they said, "Sing us one of the songs of Zion!"

So do not fear, for I am with you;
do not be dismayed, for I am your God.
I will strengthen you and help you;
I will uphold you with my
Righteous right hand.

Isaiah 41:10

A loyal, trusted, often unseen associate can be referred to by an officer or leader as their "right hand." To accomplish a shared purpose, they coordinate ahead of time the plans, schedule, personnel, and resources needed for their mission. Similarly, but with far more eternal purposes at stake, Jesus is, for us, God the Father's righteous right hand. By His crucifixion and resurrection, Jesus fulfilled God's purpose: our redemption and forgiveness from sin.

Jesus' pre-incarnate presence with the Father is validated by King David as he reflects on God with confidence: *Because you are my help, I sing in the shadow of your wings. My soul clings to you; your right hand upholds me.* (Psalm 63:7-8). Paul later confirms the power of God's right hand when he prays that believers might know the hope of God's calling and His *incomparably great power....the working of His mighty strength, which he exerted in Christ when he raised him from the dead and seated him at His right hand in the heavenly realms.* (Ephesians 1:18-20)

Are fears or dismays sapping your strength today? Take your situation before the Lord. Using the key verse above, put your name after every "you." God promises His righteous right hand will be with you, will strengthen you, will help you and uphold you. *For I am the Lord your God, who takes hold of your right hand and says to you, "Do not fear, I will help you."* (Isaiah 41:13) Believe God's word. Ask His help. Seek His answers. Picture Jesus forever at the Father's right hand.

THANK GOD: John 1:1-3 ▪ Galatians 1:3-5 ▪ Colossians 1:15-17
TRUST GOD: Psalm 73:23-24 ▪ Psalm 60:5 ▪ Philippians 2:5-7

Thank God:

John 1:1-3
In the beginning was the Word, and the Word was with God, and the Word was God. He was with God in the beginning. Through him all things were made; without him nothing was made that has been made.

Galatians 1:3-5
Grace and peace to you from God our Father and the Lord Jesus Christ, who gave himself for our sins to rescue us from the present evil age, according to the will of our God and Father, to whom be glory for ever and ever. Amen.

Colossians 1:15-17
The Son is the image of the invisible God, the firstborn over all creation. For in him all things were created: things in heaven and on earth, visible and invisible, whether thrones or powers or rulers or authorities; all things have been created through him and for him. He is before all things, and in him all things hold together.

Trust God:

Psalm 73:23-24
Yet I am always with you; you hold me by my right hand. You guide me with your counsel, and afterward you will take me into glory.

Psalm 60:5
Save us and help us with your right hand, that those you love may be delivered.

Philippians 2:5-7
In your relationships with one another, have the same mindset as Christ Jesus: Who, being in very nature God, did not consider equality with God something to be used to his own advantage; rather, he made himself nothing by taking the very nature of a servant, being made in human likeness.

I will give you a new heart and
put a new spirit in you;
I will remove from you your heart
of stone and give you a heart of flesh.

Ezekiel 36:26

The prophet-priest Ezekiel, called to minister to Hebrew exiles in Babylon, first proclaimed divine judgment against Israel. God's people had chosen idolatry over the worship of the Lord God Almighty, who had blessed them as a holy nation. Exile to Babylonia was a severe, serious consequence of their choices. But as years passed, Ezekiel's message shifted to a word of hope from their compassionate, gracious God about renewal and future restoration. That hope would one day be extended beyond Israel to all God would call to Himself in the person of Jesus. This exchange of hearts of stone for hearts of flesh, fed by God's Spirit, is how we begin to learn what kind of heart pleases our Lord.

Hearts of flesh are described in Scripture based on choices made by faith in God's word as life unfolds: cheerful, joyful, glad, grateful, pure, broken and contrite, steadfast, undivided, wise, and discerning. Hearts of stone just do what comes naturally rather than seeking to please the Lord: grumbling, grudging, judging, foolish, deceitful, hardened, darkened, calloused....hearts that need an exchange only God can provide. Which group of adjectives best characterizes your heart today?

Any heart can become anxious, fearful, wounded, aching, or troubled. But the heart of flesh can ask God's Spirit to be a calmer, a comforter, a healer, a revealer of truth. The Holy Spirit has power over whatever has befallen or befuddled us. Have you ever asked God to give you that new heart and spirit that pleases Him? Let today be that day!

THANK GOD: Matthew 5:8 ▪ Proverbs 17:22 ▪ Proverbs 12:25
TRUST GOD: Psalm 51:10,17 ▪ Jeremiah 17:9 ▪ Hebrews 3:7-8,12-13

Thank God:

Matthew 5:8
Blessed are the pure in heart, for they will see God.

Proverbs 17:22
A cheerful heart is good medicine, but a crushed spirit dries up the bones.

Proverbs 12:25
Anxiety weighs down the heart, but a kind word cheers it up.

Trust God:

Psalm 51:10, 17
Create in me a pure heart, O God, and renew a steadfast spirit within me.

My sacrifice, O God, is a broken spirit; a broken and contrite heart you, God, will not despise.

Jeremiah 17:9
The heart is deceitful above all things and beyond cure. Who can understand it?

Hebrews 3:7-8, 12-13
So, as the Holy Spirit says: "Today, if you hear his voice, do not harden your hearts as you did in the rebellion, during the time of testing in the wilderness."

See to it, brothers and sisters, that none of you has a sinful, unbelieving heart that turns away from the living God. But encourage one another daily, as long as it is called "Today," so that none of you may be hardened by sin's deceitfulness.

Abram believed the Lord, and He credited it to him as righteousness.

Genesis 15:6 Romans 4:3

A fascinating discovery about the Bible is the referencing of people and truths between the Old and New Testaments. One verse or passage is substantiated or clarified by another. For instance, God's concept of righteousness....exactly who are the righteous in God's eyes?

"Being right" all the time does not make one righteous. Nor does striving for your "rights" or proclaiming oneself righteous make it so. *All have sinned and fall short of the glory of God,* so perfection is not a requirement. None are righteous on their own....not by wealth, not by strength, luck, beauty, hard work, or a strict moral code. So how did Abram (renamed Abraham by God) come to be declared righteous? He believed God's word of promise to him regarding a son. The basis of Abram's righteousness was his faith that God's word to him was true.

Today, millennia later, we still become righteous only by faith when we believe God's word to us about another son, His own Son, the Lord Jesus Christ. The gospel of Jesus Christ is *the power of God for the salvation of everyone who believes. For in the gospel a righteousness that is from God is revealed, a righteousness that is by faith from first to last...the righteous will live by faith.* If by faith you believe God's words in Scripture about Jesus, crucified, dead, buried and risen....then He declares you righteous. *This righteousness from God comes through faith in Jesus Christ to all who believe.* You may already believe <u>in God</u>, but be like righteous Abraham and <u>believe God</u> for His word and promise to <u>you</u>.

THANK GOD: Romans 4:19-25 ▪ II Corinthians 5:21 ▪ Hebrews 11:7
TRUST GOD: Psalm 37:16,25,39 ▪ Romans 1:16-17 ▪ Romans 3:22-24

Thank God:

Romans 4:20-24
Yet he did not waver through unbelief regarding the promise of God, but was strengthened in his faith and gave glory to God, being fully persuaded that God had power to do what he had promised. This is why "it was credited to him as righteousness." The words "it was credited to him" were written not for him alone, but also for us, to whom God will credit righteousness—for us who believe in him who raised Jesus our Lord from the dead.

II Corinthians 5:21
God made him who had no sin to be sin for us, so that in him we might become the righteousness of God.

Hebrews 11:7
By faith Noah, when warned about things not yet seen, in holy fear built an ark to save his family. By his faith he condemned the world and became heir of the righteousness that is in keeping with faith.

Trust God:

Psalm 37:39
The salvation of the righteous comes from the Lord; he is their stronghold in time of trouble.

Romans 1:16-17
For I am not ashamed of the gospel, because it is the power of God that brings salvation to everyone who believes: first to the Jew, then to the Gentile. For in the gospel the righteousness of God is revealed—a righteousness that is by faith from first to last, just as it is written: "The righteous will live by faith."

Romans 3:22-24
This righteousness is given through faith in Jesus Christ to all who believe. There is no difference between Jew and Gentile, for all have sinned and fall short of the glory of God, and all are justified freely by his grace through the redemption that came by Christ Jesus.

But God chose the foolish things....
the weak things...the lowly things....
so that no one may boast before him.

I Corinthians 1:27-28

My message...was not with wise
and persuasive words, but with a
demonstration of the Spirit's power,
so that your faith might not rest on
men's wisdom, but on God's power.

I Corinthians 2:4-5

Do you ever try to figure out what the Lord is doing in your life? Scripture clearly reminds us that God's thoughts and ways are always higher than ours. In fact, we are told that His paths are "beyond tracing out." So we should not be surprised that God's word will often have a <u>so that</u> to indicate clearly His desired response from us.

God's ways may seem foolish to many: Jesus came as a baby, a picture of weakness. God's Son, the King of Kings, was crucified, killed by the cruelest form of punishment known. The Apostle Paul asked this rhetorical question, "Has God not made foolish the wisdom of the world?" The demonstration of God's power when He raised Jesus from the grave reveals His gift of love and redemption from our worst fears .....death and separation from God because of our sin. The message of the cross is the power of God, though the world's wise may believe not.

No one can boast about being stronger or wiser than God, nor can anyone brag about earning the Savior's gift. Those who bring the good news of the Gospel must do so in humility, pointing not to the cleverness of their words or their power of persuasion....but simply telling others what Jesus has done on their behalf, <u>so that</u> they, too, can rest their faith on the power of God rather than their own wisdom!

THANK GOD: Isaiah 55:8-9 ▪ I Corinthians 1:20-21 ▪ Ephesians 2:8-9
TRUST GOD: I Corinthians 2:9-10 ▪ Colossians 1:9-10 ▪ Romans 11:33

Thank God:

Isaiah 55:8-9

*"For my thoughts are not your thoughts, neither are your ways my ways,"
declares the Lord. "As the heavens are higher than the earth, so are my
ways higher than your ways and my thoughts than your thoughts."*

I Corinthians 1:20-21

*Where is the wise person? Where is the teacher of the law? Where is the
philosopher of this age? Has not God made foolish the wisdom of the world?
For since in the wisdom of God the world through its wisdom did not know
him, God was pleased through the foolishness of what was preached to
save those who believe.*

Ephesians 2:8-9

*For it is by grace you have been saved, through faith—and this is not from
yourselves, it is the gift of God—not by works, so that no one can boast.*

Trust God:

I Corinthians 2:9-10

*However, as it is written: "What no eye has seen, what no ear has heard,
and what no human mind has conceived"—the things God has prepared
for those who love him—these are the things God has revealed to us by his
Spirit. The Spirit searches all things, even the deep things of God.*

Colossians 1:9-10

*For this reason, since the day we heard about you, we have not stopped
praying for you. We continually ask God to fill you with the knowledge of
his will through all the wisdom and understanding that the Spirit gives, so
that you may live a life worthy of the Lord and please him in every way:
bearing fruit in every good work, growing in the knowledge of God...*

Romans 11:33

*Oh, the depth of the riches of the wisdom and knowledge of God! How
unsearchable his judgments, and his paths beyond tracing out!*

Be on guard; stand firm in the faith; be men of courage; be strong. Do everything in love.

I Corinthians 16:13-14

A combat platoon was running in retreat toward their foxholes under heavy fire. When a soldier realized his best friend had been shot and was still in the field, he readied himself to rescue his buddy. The officer in charge disparaged him, forbidding him to take such a risk. But the determined soldier ran back onto the battlefield, calling his friend's name. A short time later he was seen hobbling back across the field, carrying the limp and bloody body of his fellow soldier. The officer upbraided him again for the foolish risk and waste of time going after a dead man, saying there was nothing he could do. But the soldier said triumphantly, "No, sir, you're wrong. You see, I got there just in time! Before he died, his last words were, 'I knew you would come.'" *

May it never be too late to show God's love to a family member or friend, or to share with a dying patient that Jesus has overcome death and given eternal life to those who trust in Him. Such a call to duty can be as scary as running across an active battlefield. The soldier's risk was a gift of loving courage to his friend. Life can be a sort of battlefield for many. The enemy may not be flesh and blood, but unseen forces of fear and discouragement, of despair and hopelessness. Will you be strong and courageous in seeking to rescue your friend or fellow worker with words of encouragement from God's truth or with loving deeds of kindness? Thanks be to God who *gives us the victory through our Lord Jesus Christ.*

THANK GOD: John 3:16 ▪ John 11:25 ▪ I Corinthians 15:57
TRUST GOD: Deuteronomy 31:6 ▪ John 16:33 ▪ II Corinthians 1:21-22

* The Treasure of a Friend, John C. Maxwell, pp. 27-28.

Thank God:

John 3:16
For God so loved the world that he gave his one and only Son, that whoever believes in him shall not perish but have eternal life.

John 11:25
Jesus said to her, "I am the resurrection and the life. The one who believes in me will live, even though they die..."

I Corinthians 15:57
But thanks be to God! He gives us the victory through our Lord Jesus Christ.

Trust God:

Deuteronomy 31:6
Be strong and courageous. Do not be afraid or terrified because of them, for the Lord your God goes with you; he will never leave you nor forsake you.

John 16:33
I have told you these things, so that in me you may have peace. In this world you will have trouble. But take heart! I have overcome the world.

II Corinthians 1:21-22
Now it is God who makes both us and you stand firm in Christ. He anointed us, set his seal of ownership on us, and put his Spirit in our hearts as a deposit, guaranteeing what is to come.

Command those who are rich....not to be arrogant nor to put their hope in wealth....but to put their hope in God who richly provides us with everything for our enjoyment.

I Timothy 6:17

Money itself is not the problem....we may have a little or a lot....but the place it occupies in our affections is what needs monitoring. Are my hopes based on God's riches or transient wealth? The most generous people are often those who give or share out of their lack, while the rich can be very stingy. Those God has entrusted with an abundance of material wealth are called to demonstrate a gift of generosity by "doing well and doing good." But did you know God may choose to make us rich in other ways, less visible perhaps, but very important to Him?

Has God chosen to make you rich in relationships? Your love of family, friends, or co-workers is felt by time spent helping or just enjoying them, cheerleading for their success, providing something needed, or simply making them feel special. Scripture speaks of a good name as being better than riches, and a reputation of high esteem being greater than silver or gold. God treasures the life of great personal integrity. Do you enjoy an "opportunity for usefulness"? Then God has made you rich in good deeds....lending a timely, helping hand, especially to someone who could never repay you. Has the Lord made you rich in faith? He often chooses those who are poor in the eyes of the world to be rich in faith, encouraging others to trust God, praising and thanking Him for daily bread and His unfailing love. God knows you and your net worth....trust Him in humility, being content with His choice of riches for you, both now and in every season of your life.

THANK GOD: Philippians 4:19 ▪ James 2:5 ▪ Proverbs 22:1
TRUST GOD: Hebrews 13:5 ▪ Psalm 62:10 ▪ I Timothy 6:6-8,10

Thank God:

Philippians 4:19
And my God will supply all of your needs according to his glorious riches in Christ Jesus.

James 2:5
Listen, my dear brothers: Has not God chosen those who are poor in the eyes of the world to be rich in faith and to inherit the kingdom he promised those who love him?

Proverbs 22:1
A good name is more desirable than great riches; to be esteemed is better than silver or gold.

Trust God:

Hebrews 13:5
Keep your lives free from the love of money and be content with what you have, because God has said. "Never will I leave you. Never will I forsake you."

Psalm 62:10
Do not trust in extortion or take pride in stolen goods. Though your riches increase, do not set you heart on them.

I Timothy 6:6-8, 10
But godliness with contentment is great gain. For we brought nothing into the world, and we can take nothing out of it. But if we have food and clothing, we will be content with that.

For the love of money is root of all kinds of evil.

*Wait for the Lord; be strong and take heart
and wait for the Lord.*

Psalm 27:14

The word HOPE has a futuristic implication. Hope is rarely instantaneously fulfilled. A "wait" factor is always associated with it. Scripture is filled with admonitions to wait, wait patiently, wait in hope. Yet few words are as dread to twenty-first century ears as WAIT. How many times have you thought, "I hate to wait!" Instant gratification, immediate results, and rapid responses are the order of the day. Still we find ourselves in waiting mode, with very important issues of our lives.

Are you waiting to hear about an application for college or a job? For the results of a medical test? A court decision or sentence? For healing of an injury or surgery? For someone to marry? For the answer to a long-time personal prayer? The wait time seems just as important to God as what we are waiting for! So how can we take heart while in God's waiting room? We can saturate our spirits with God's Word.

Let God's everlasting arms uphold you while you wait. He may want to change your perspective. He may use the wait time to work behind the scenes on your behalf in some unimaginable way. The wait may be about God's preparing another person to fulfill His will for you. Waiting can be a time of strengthening faith muscles with prayer, perseverance, and endurance. Pray as you read your Bible. God may use you as an example of what waiting patiently without losing heart looks like.

We wait in certain hope that the Sovereign Lord wants His best for us. He has made us, loves us, sent Jesus to redeem us. Now He wants to conform us to His image....and that could take a while!

THANK GOD: Deuteronomy 33:27 ▪ Psalm 40:1-3 ▪ Isaiah 30:18
TRUST GOD: Psalm 33:20-22 ▪ Psalm 130:5-6 ▪ Romans 8:29

Thank God:

Deuteronomy 33:27
The eternal God is your refuge, and underneath are the everlasting arms. He will drive out your enemies before you, saying, 'Destroy them!'

Psalm 40:1-3
I waited patiently for the Lord; he turned to me and heard my cry. He lifted me out of the slimy pit, out of the mud and mire; he set my feet on a rock and gave me a firm place to stand. He put a new song in my mouth, a hymn of praise to our God. Many will see and fear the Lord and put their trust in him.

Isaiah 30:18
Yet the Lord longs to be gracious to you; therefore he will rise up to show you compassion. For the Lord is a God of justice. Blessed are all who wait for him!

Trust God:

Psalm 33:20-22
We wait in hope for the Lord; he is our help and our shield. In him our hearts rejoice, for we trust in his holy name. May your unfailing love be with us, Lord, even as we put our hope in you.

Psalm 130:5-6
I wait for the Lord, my whole being waits, and in his word I put my hope. I wait for the Lord more than watchmen wait for the morning, more than watchmen wait for the morning.

Romans 8:29
For those God foreknew he also predestined to be conformed to the image of his Son, that he might be the firstborn among many brothers and sisters.

Without faith it is impossible to please God,
because anyone who comes to him
must believe he exists
and that he rewards those who earnestly seek him.

Hebrews 11:6

Faith is a complete trust or confident belief in someone or something. Faith in God means believing in His existence even though articulating proof is difficult. The proverbial "leap of faith" means God's Spirit is calling you to acknowledge Him as you read His words in the Bible or are stirred by the testimony or example of others. One hymn writer put it this way: "I know not how this saving faith / To me He did impart, / Nor how believing in His word / Wrought peace within my heart / I know not how the Spirit moves, / Convincing men of sin, / Revealing Jesus through the word, / Creating faith in Him." * Faith is God's gift.

The Bible invites us to be confident that God exists and wants us to seek <u>Him</u> personally, not just do good deeds we think He might like. Our faith pleases Him, and He rewards earnest believers. There is no dishonor in desiring God's reward. Who does not know about rewards/points systems in every business today, promising material rewards for frequent spending? But God's rewards are mostly in the unseen and eternal realm....rewards that far outweigh those of temporal value: abundant life, peace that passes understanding, grace sufficient for every need, joy and peace in believing, eternal life....those are some of the rewards for faithful seekers of the Lord God Almighty. Are you among them? If not, ask Him today for that faith that pleases Him.

THANK GOD: Psalm 31:19 KJV ▪ Ephesians 2:9-10 ▪ Philippians 4:6-7
TRUST GOD: Hebrews 11:1 ▪ I Corinthians 2:4-5 ▪ II Corinthians 9:8

* David W. Whittle, "I Know Whom I Have Believed," v. 2, 3.

Thank God:

Psalm 31:19 KJV
For those God foreknew he also predestined to be conformed to the image of his Son, that he might be the firstborn among many brothers and sisters.

Ephesians 2:9-10
Not of works, lest any man should boast. For we are his workmanship, created in Christ Jesus unto good works, which God hath before ordained that we should walk in them.

Philippians 4:6-7
Do not be anxious about anything, but in every situation, by prayer and petition, with thanksgiving, present your requests to God. And the peace of God, which transcends all understanding, will guard your hearts and your minds in Christ Jesus.

Trust God:

Hebrews 11:1
Now faith is confidence in what we hope for and assurance about what we do not see.

I Corinthians 2:4-5
My message and my preaching were not with wise and persuasive words, but with a demonstration of the Spirit's power, so that your faith might not rest on human wisdom, but on God's power.

II Corinthians 9:8
And God is able to bless you abundantly, so that in all things at all times, having all that you need, you will abound in every good work.

*Be strong and take heart, all you
that hope in the Lord.*

Psalm 31:24

Do you ever post notes to yourself so you will not forget an appointment or some item at the store? Forgetfulness is common to all of us, creating regrets and requiring apologies. Just as we use memory joggers for our daily schedules, our hearts need reminders that the Lord is the One in whom our hopes are never misplaced or forgotten. His Word constantly gives exhortations to "be strong" and "take heart."

Because our memories tend to be short, a crisis can quickly erase recall of God's past faithfulness to us. Illness, pain, anxiety, or a sudden loss cause our imaginations to run wild with fear about our ability to cope or recover. People we love disappoint us; our confidence is undermined by self-doubts; our hopes are dashed by events completely out of our control; chronic conditions flair up with a vengeance. Joy and peace vanish from our minds. In these hard times, hold on to hope by turning to the God of Hope. Thank Him for promising He will never leave you or forsake you. Call out to Him in your despair and stress to calm your heart, so that you can remember He loves you. Take heart! Ask for God's wisdom, trust Him, then listen for His voice, looking for comfort and encouragement from Him. Be strong! You are not alone!

Pray Psalm 31:7 back to the Lord: *I will be glad and rejoice in your love, for you saw my affliction and knew the anguish of my soul.* Rest your heart in His unfailing love. Trust His faithfulness once again. Return to hope and the joy and peace of the Spirit, in believing God's promises!

THANK GOD: Psalm 28:7 ▪ Psalm 56:4 ▪ Romans 15:13
TRUST GOD: Deuteronomy 31:8 ▪ Psalm 27:14 ▪ Psalm 32:10

Thank God:

Psalm 28:7
The Lord is my strength and my shield; my heart trusts in him, and he helps me. My heart leaps for joy, and with my song I praise him.

Psalm 56:4
In God, whose word I praise—in God I trust and am not afraid. What can mere mortals do to me?

Romans 15:13
May the God of hope fill you with all joy and peace as you trust in him, so that you may overflow with hope by the power of the Holy Spirit.

Trust God:

Deuteronomy 31:8
The Lord himself goes before you and will be with you; he will never leave you nor forsake you. Do not be afraid; do not be discouraged.

Psalm 27:14
Wait for the Lord; be strong and take heart and wait for the Lord.

Psalm 32:10
Many are the woes of the wicked, but the Lord's unfailing love surrounds the one who trusts in him.

..... take note of this: Everyone should be quick to listen, slow to speak, and slow to become angry....

James 1:19

A TV travel show, spotlighting a location known as Cowboy-Town USA, featured the locals in a gathering place dancing the Texas two-step. Well done, the dance looks like an effortless glide of couples perfectly in sync, magically covering an expansive floor with smooth, fascinating precision. Observers wanting to join in inquire about the basics to dancing the two-step. In dance talk, the reply was always "Slow, slow, quick, quick" or the reverse, "quick, quick, slow, slow."

But wait....here is a word-association discovery to help me recall three Bible instructions important for living every day God's way. I should always be *quick* to listen, *slow* to speak, *slow* to anger. The admonition to listen is first, reminding me to make that my quickest response. Being doubly quick to listen is in order before any reaction! Listening is twice as important as speaking. After all, the Lord gave me two ears and only one mouth....that I may be quick, quick to listen to whomever I encounter in conversation.

Conversely, may I be slow to speak....thinking about what to say and praying silently for gentleness and humility, especially if my response is to disagree or confront. Prayer helps me be slow to become angry. Wrath risks relationships, spoils a chance for witness. So, Lord, let the Texas two-step pattern, quick, quick, slow, slow, be a guide for my interactions and reactions....that my great joy would be dancing in sync with your Word, inviting others to put on their dancing shoes, too!

THANK GOD: Psalm 119:11,14-15 ▪ Psalm 149:3 ▪ Proverbs 18:13
TRUST GOD: Psalm 19:14 ▪ Proverbs 15:1,19:20 ▪ James 1:20,26

Thank God:

Psalm 119:11, 14-15
I have hidden your word in my heart that I might not sin against you.

I rejoice in following your statutes as one rejoices in great riches. I meditate on your precepts and consider your ways.

Psalm 149:3
Let them praise his name with dancing and make music to him with timbrel and harp.

Proverbs 18:13
To answer before listening—that is folly and shame.

Trust God:

Psalm 19:14
Houses and wealth are inherited from parents, but a prudent wife is from the Lord.

Proverbs 15:1, 19:20
A gentle answer turns away wrath, but a harsh word stirs up anger.

James 1:20, 26
...because human anger does not produce the righteousness that God desires.

Those who consider themselves religious and yet do not keep a tight rein on their tongues deceive themselves, and their religion is worthless.

Commit your way unto the Lord; trust also in him, and He will act.

Psalm 37:5 ESV

A devotional word from Amy Carmichael on this verse has greatly encouraged me when facing pressures, decisions, or stress. (As God's early 20th century missionary to India, Amy could be profiled today as a heroic rescuer of girls being "trafficked" for exploitation.) The Hebrew word for <u>commit</u> can be translated "roll your way upon." Carmichael's encouragement was to "Roll everything that concerns you upon the Lord." * Before long, God showed me an illustration of this truth….how much easier it is to roll a heavy burden than try to carry it alone.

A very large oak limb had somehow settled onto the roof of my house. Tree surgeons began removing pieces of the huge branch from atop the roof. Suddenly, they realized the main branch had actually cracked from the trunk, and the bulk of this century-old tree came crashing from the roof to the ground. The giant log had to be sawed into multiple round chunks too heavy to be lifted, even by two people. But the foreman assured me that he would be able to roll them alone, all the way to the curb for pick-up. Rolling weighty loads from one place to another is a major moving method for what is too heavy to be lifted or carried….whether heavy logs or personal life burdens.

When next your shoulders feel the weight of cares, snares, trials, or stress, prayerfully "roll your way upon the Lord." Trust Him to act. His action may happen at once or be orchestrated later by His hidden hand. Let God be your burden bearer by rolling your way upon Him.

THANK GOD: Psalm 68:19 ▪ Proverbs 16:3 ▪ Matthew 11:28-30
TRUST GOD: Psalm 55:17, 22 ▪ Proverbs 3:5-6 ▪ I Peter 5:7

* Amy Carmichael, <u>Edges of His Ways: Selections from Notes of Amy Carmichael</u>, CLC Publications, 1955, p. 75.

Thank God:

Psalm 68:19
Praise be to the Lord, to God our Savior, who daily bears our burdens.

Proverbs 16:3
Commit to the Lord whatever you do, and he will establish your plans.

Matthew 11:28-30
Come to me, all you who are weary and burdened, and I will give you rest. Take my yoke upon you and learn from me, for I am gentle and humble in heart, and you will find rest for your souls. For my yoke is easy and my burden is light.

Trust God:

Psalm 55:17, 22
Evening, morning and noon I cry out in distress, and he hears my voice.

Cast your cares on the Lord and he will sustain you; he will never let the righteous be shaken.

Proverbs 3:5-6
Trust in the Lord with all your heart and lean not on your own understanding; in all your ways acknowledge him and he will make your paths straight.

I Peter 5:7
Cast all your anxiety on him because he cares for you.

The Lord is thy keeper....

Psalm 121:5 KJV

You will keep in perfect peace him whose mind is steadfast, because he trusts in you.

Isaiah 26:3

Has anyone ever asked you to keep something for them? Keep a secret or surprise? Keep a promise? Keep them in your prayers? "Keeping" implies relationship. You trust the one you ask to keep something on your behalf. But God takes "keeping power" to another level. He is the ultimate "keeper"....watching over you at the same time He is giving you peace when your focus is on Him. The Priestly Blessing, *The Lord bless you and keep you* ends with *and give you peace.* Have you ever entrusted yourself to God's keeping?

The Psalmists sought God's keeping power in their lives: *Keep my lamp burning.* (18:28) *Keep your servant from willful sin.* (19:13) *Keep me from harm.* (121:7) *Keep watch over the door of my lips.* (141:3) Ask God specifically for your need of His keeping power. My dear mother would daily pray, "Lord, keep me sweet and on my feet." Amen!

We entrust ourselves to God's keeping power when we trust His promises, then seek His power to obey His commands. Who but God could make obedience appealing, even to a resistant heart, by pledging that in keeping His instructions, there is great reward? (Ps.19:11) Scoffers will belittle God's promise-keeping, and we may battle doubts about our own perseverance. By faith, we need to move on by declaring these words: *I know whom I have believed, and I am persuaded that he is able to keep that which I have committed to him against that day.* Whether it be today, tomorrow, or my last day, the Lord is my keeper!

THANK GOD: Numbers 6:24-26 ▪ Jude 24 ▪ I Peter 1:3-4
TRUST GOD: I Chronicles 29:18 ▪ Isaiah 26:3 ▪ II Timothy 1:12 KJV

Thank God:

Numbers 6:24-26
The Lord bless you and keep you; the Lord make his face shine on you and be gracious to you; the Lord turn his face toward you and give you peace.

Jude 24
To him who is able to keep you from stumbling and to present you before his glorious presence without fault and with great joy...

I Peter 1:3-4
Praise be to the God and Father of our Lord Jesus Christ! In his great mercy he has given us new birth into a living hope through the resurrection of Jesus Christ from the dead, and into an inheritance that can never perish, spoil, or fade—kept in heaven for you.

Trust God:

I Chronicles 29:18
Lord, the God of our fathers Abraham, Isaac and Israel, keep these desires and thoughts in the hearts of your people forever, and keep their hearts loyal to you.

Isaiah 26:3 KJV
Thou wilt keep him in perfect peace whose mind is stayed on thee; because he trusteth in thee.

II Timothy 1:12 KJV
....for I know whom I have believed, and am persuaded that he is able to keep that which I have committed unto him against that day.

*With man this is impossible, but with God
all things are possible.*

Matthew 19:26

For nothing is impossible with God.

Luke 1:37

If ever there were a truth to generate hope in a human heart, it is that the Sovereign Lord is also the God of the Impossible. Do you have an impossible hope? A need no person can meet? Would you in faith entrust your impossible situation to God....with no timetable, no stipulations or demands? (God well knows our impatience!) Will you write or bookmark your hope beside a verse in your Bible, then thank and trust God for what He can and will do?

For those who do not yet know that nothing is impossible for God, hopelessness can be inevitable. But even a small word of hope from a friend can make a tremendous difference. At a funeral remembrance for a very brave lady who had survived a liver transplant for 19 years, the pastor related a condolence message just received by her family. The sender recalled in his own life a time when he had been told he was dying. When he called my friend to tell her he was terminal, she said simply, "That's not necessarily so." Her story was her evidence. The writer expressed to the family that hers were the first words of hope anyone had offered him, and it meant the world to him. Thankfully, my friend spoke rightly....the sender was still living! Are you a friend who listens for opportunity to bring hope to another? That is exactly what God does for us when we need hope. He leads us to His word: *Is anything too hard for the Lord?* (Genesis 18:14)

THANK GOD: Isaiah 55:8 ▪ Jeremiah 32:17,27 ▪ Philippians 4:19
TRUST GOD: Proverbs 3:5-6 ▪ Psalm 37:3-4 ▪ Romans 4:18

Thank God:

Isaiah 55:8
"For my thoughts are not your thoughts, neither are your ways my ways,"
declares the Lord.

Jeremiah 32:17, 27
Ah, Sovereign Lord, you have made the heavens and the earth by your
great power and outstretched arm. Nothing is too hard for you.

"I am the Lord, the God of all mankind. Is anything too hard for me?"

Philippians 4:19
And my God will meet all your needs according to the riches of his glory in
Christ Jesus.

Trust God:

Proverbs 3:5-6
Trust in the Lord with all your heart and lean not on your own under-
standing; in all your ways acknowledge him and he will make your
paths straight.

Psalm 37:3-4
Trust in the Lord and do good; dwell in the land and enjoy safe pasture.
Take delight in the Lord, and he will give you the desires of your heart.

Romans 4:18
Against all hope, Abraham in hope believed and so became the father of
many nations, just as it had been said to him, "So shall your offspring be."

Hope deferred makes the heart sick, but
a longing fulfilled....is sweet to the soul.

Proverbs 13:12, 19

Sick, aching, broken....does that describe your heart condition? Even if the physical heart is still beating, the spiritual or emotional health of our hearts can be compromised by grief or disappointment, by deferred or dashed hopes, or by sin, needing forgiveness. When prayer seems to go unanswered, or our personal longings are unfulfilled, rather than asking, "Where is God?" try thanking Him that He is still the God of love, peace, comfort, grace, forgiveness, and hope....even when present situations or longings seem to indicate otherwise. God never changes, and nothing is too hard for Him. (Jeremiah 32:17)

As you are thankful in prayer to your heavenly Father, implore Him to be working behind the scenes in your behalf, to be "engineering circumstances," as Oswald Chambers liked to say, or shaping time and events to favor you and your situation. God is able to do more to overcome heart sickness than we could ever ask or think when His Spirit is at work in us to forgive and be forgiven, and to show us that thanking and trusting the Lord is a key to recovery or healing.

A caring person is often part of God's answer to the fatigue and lethargy of a sick heart....one who has learned the power and proof of this modern proverb: "Energy is more than doubled by a dose of hope and cheerfulness." (Verdell Kidder) Ask God for a friend with a merry, cheerful heart....one whose hopeful words will prove to be better than a medicine, sweeter than honey to your soul, and safer than a toxic tonic.

THANK GOD: Psalm 51:17 ▪ Proverbs 12:18,25 ▪ Ephesians 3:20
TRUST GOD: Psalm 119:116 ▪ Psalm 51:10 ▪ Proverbs 15:23

Thank God:

Psalm 51:17
My sacrifice, O God, is a broken spirit; a broken and contrite heart you, God, will not despise.

Proverbs 12:25
Anxiety weighs down the heart, but a kind word cheers it up.

Ephesians 3:20
Now to him who is able to do immeasurably more than all we ask or imagine, according to his power that is at work within us...

Trust God:

Psalm 119:116
Sustain me, my God, according to your promise, and I will live; do not let my hopes be dashed.

Psalm 51:10
Create in me a pure heart, O God, and renew a steadfast spirit within me.

Proverbs 15:18, 23
A hot-tempered person stirs up conflict, but the one who is patient calms a quarrel.

A person finds joy in giving an apt reply—and how good is a timely word!

You are my hiding place; you will protect
me from trouble and surround me with
songs of deliverance.

Psalm 32:7

Very few of us will ever have to go into hiding to be safe. But anyone who has read Corrie ten Boom's book <u>The Hiding Place</u> will forever connect this verse with her family's experience during World War II hiding Jewish refugees in their Holland home. Their courageous story gives amazing wisdom and insight into what it means to trust God completely, and to learn to give thanks when the worst of circumstances surrounds you. God, indeed, became Corrie's hiding place, even as her family home provided one for those fleeing death in gas chambers. No matter the distress or trouble, God can become our hiding place, too.

Are you embarrassed over a personal failure? Are you in a place of total anxiety or confusion about the future? Are you somehow in harm's way? You may know the Lord has promised to be with you always, but have you ever thought of His presence as a hiding place? God can be that for you and me according to this truth: *Thou shall hide them in the secret of thy presence from the pride of man; thou shalt keep them secretly in a pavilion from the strife of tongues. (Ps. 31:20 KJV)* A pavilion of His presence is the safest place to take refuge and seek protection. And God, being always better than we know, even provides soothing songs of deliverance to surround us while we are in hiding.

God's songs reveal His unfailing love encircling those who trust in Him. His favor surrounds us as a shield, and His presence is our hiding place. Let His songs nourish you as you seek and hide in Him.

THANK GOD: Psalm 5:12 ▪ Psalm 27:5 ▪ Psalm 31:24
TRUST GOD: Psalm 17:8 ▪ Psalm 143:9 ▪ Proverbs 28:12

Thank God:

Psalm 5:12
Surely, Lord, you bless the righteous; you surround them with your favor as with a shield.

Psalm 27:5
For in the day of trouble he will keep me safe in his dwelling; he will hide me in the shelter of his sacred tent and set me high upon a rock.

Psalm 31:24
Be strong and take heart, all you who hope in the Lord.

Trust God:

Psalm 17:8
Keep me as the apple of your eye; hide me in the shadow of your wings...

Psalm 143:9
Rescue me from my enemies, Lord, for I hide myself in you.

Proverbs 28:12
When the righteous triumph, there is great elation; but when the wicked rise to power, people go into hiding.

The Lord your God is with you, He is mighty to save. He will take great delight in you....quiet you with his love.... rejoice over you with singing.

Zephaniah 3:17

Can you picture yourself as God's child, "swinging in the hammock of His love"? God Almighty is with you, delighting in you. His calming love quiets your heart as you gently swing back and forth. You can even hear singing. But Zephaniah, the prophet, has just announced a coming judgment against Israel's Southern Kingdom for unrepentant idolatry and failure to seek the Lord. So why this picture of quiet contentment? Whenever God's prophets forecast His wrath, words of comforting hope and promises of restoration are spoken for those who, in humility, have obeyed Him and have sought His righteousness in true worship.

With any mention today of a coming judgment, the cultural tendency is either to laugh in derision or to resort to the porch of self-pity, where a litany of seemingly unfair, undeserved, uncontrollable life factors are rehearsed and blamed for deliberate disobedience to God. The blame game results from failure to take responsibility for poor choices. In those moments of arrogance, brooding or bitterness, may we confess to God a desire for change and humble ourselves before Him in repentance. He will hear and care for us, gently inviting us to join those who already know the joy of "swinging in the hammock of His love."

God's mercy and grace can move us from hostilities to resting in His presence, experiencing His delight, with a heart quieted by His love....hearing His song of rejoicing over our renewal and restoration.

THANK GOD: Deuteronomy 30:8-9 ▪ Psalm 32:7 ▪ James 4:6-7,10
TRUST GOD: Psalm 51:16-17 ▪ Zephaniah 3:12 ▪ I Peter 5:6-7

Thank God:

Deuteronomy 30:8-9
You will again obey the Lord and follow all his commands I am giving you today. Then the Lord your God will make you most prosperous in all the work of your hands and in the fruit of your womb, the young of your live-stock and the crops of your land. The Lord will again delight in you and make you prosperous, just as he delighted in your ancestors...

Psalm 32:7
You are my hiding place; you will protect me from trouble and surround me with songs of deliverance.

James 4:6-7, 10
But he gives us more grace. That is why Scripture says: "God opposes the proud but shows favor to the humble." Submit yourselves, then, to God. Resist the devil, and he will flee from you.

Humble yourselves before the Lord, and he will lift you up.

Trust God:

Psalm 51:16-17
You do not delight in sacrifice, or I would bring it; you do not take plea-sure in burnt offerings. My sacrifice, O God, is a broken spirit; a broken and contrite heart you, God, will not despise.

Zephaniah 3:12
But I will leave within you the meek and humble. The remnant of Israel will trust in the name of the Lord.

I Peter 5:6-7
Humble yourselves, therefore, under God's mighty hand, that he may lift you up in due time. Cast all your anxiety on him because he cares for you.

*We wait in hope for the Lord; he is our hope
and our shield.*

Psalm 33:20

While waiting in hope, let your heart be encouraged by Scriptural pictures of God as a <u>shield</u>. In this century, the word itself brings to mind Medieval knights on horseback, each holding a large, protective apparatus featuring a colorful or symbolic design. The shield's purpose was to protect a warrior or knight from the direct blows of an enemy's weapon. But shields were in use long before the Middle Ages. God spoke to the Patriarch Abraham a promise to *be his shield and his very great reward.* Ever thought of praying for God to be your shield?

Israel's King David knew God as his shield. In Psalms of praise, as well as desperation, he often called the Lord his shield....a providential protection that guards body, mind, and spirit from the blows of an enemy, visible or invisible. *But you are a shield around me, O Lord. He is a shield for all who take refuge in him.* David also connected God's shield with blessing....surrounding the righteous with His favor as a shield. Who would not desire to be surrounded with God's favor?

Flashing forward to the New Testament, the Apostle Paul's word picture in Ephesians of believers putting on "the whole armor of God" includes taking "the shield of faith" with which we can extinguish the fiery darts of the enemy. Ever felt as if you were in the cross-hairs of fiery darts? Take the shield of your faith in Christ Jesus, who alone is our hope, and call on God to surround you with His protection, His favor, and His blessing.

THANK GOD: Genesis 6:8, 15:1 ▪ Psalm 18:30 ▪ Exodus 34:9
TRUST GOD: Psalm 3:3, 5:12 ▪ Psalm 28:7 ▪ Ephesians 6:13-17

Thank God:

Genesis 6:8, 15:1
But Noah found favor in the eyes of the Lord.

After this, the word of the Lord came to Abram in a vision: "Do not be afraid, Abram. I am your shield, your very great reward."

Psalm 18:30
As for God, his way is perfect: The Lord's word is flawless; he shields all who take refuge in him.

Exodus 34:9
"Lord," he said, "if I have found favor in your eyes, then let the Lord go with us. Although this is a stiff-necked people, forgive our wickedness and our sin, and take us as your inheritance."

Trust God:

Psalm 3:3, 5:12
But you, Lord, are a shield around me, my glory, the One who lifts my head high.

Surely, Lord, you bless the righteous; you surround them with your favor as with a shield.

Psalm 28:7
The Lord is my strength and my shield; my heart trusts in him, and he helps me. My heart leaps for joy, and with my song I praise him.

Ephesians 6:13-17
Therefore put on the full armor of God, so that when the day of evil comes, you may be able to stand your ground, and after you have done everything, to stand. Stand firm then, with the belt of truth buckled around your waist, with the breastplate of righteousness in place, and with your feet fitted with the readiness that comes from the gospel of peace. In addition to all this, take up the shield of faith, with which you can extinguish all the flaming arrows of the evil one. Take the helmet of salvation and the sword of the Spirit, which is the word of God.

I know that my Redeemer lives, and that in the end he will stand upon the earth.

Job 19:25

Redemption always involves an exchange. Today we can use "rewards" points to exchange for a plane ticket, gift cards, or a much-desired item too expensive for limited discretionary income. We like the process because it appears to cost us nothing. But in the spiritual realm, the cost of redemption is not point accumulation but the life of God's Son. Jesus was sent to die sacrificially that He might exchange death for life in all who put their faith in His atoning love, thanking God for His gift of eternal life. His followers soon learned He is also able to redeem sorrow and losses in their lives, working all things together for the good of those who love Him. (Romans 8:28) Let this be new hope for believers endlessly wrestling with failures, unforgiveness, mistakes, disappointments, or regrets resulting from sin, poor choices, or shirked responsibilities. Know, like Job, that your Redeemer lives.

Destitute of everything but his knowledge and trust of God, Job spoke in faith about his Redeemer standing on the earth....a forecast of the coming of Jesus, not only as Savior for sinners, but as a Redeemer, a defender of His own when they despair even of life itself. Today after Jesus' advent, crucifixion, death, resurrection, and ascension, we know our Savior, our Redeemer, lives. For now we are waiting in hope for Jesus to stand again upon the earth in His second coming....in glorious victory and vindication of His own who know Him as Lord, Savior and Redeemer, trusting Him for life abundant now and life eternal to come.

THANK GOD: Genesis 50:20 ▪ Psalm 103:1-4 ▪ Romans 6:23
TRUST GOD: Isaiah 43:1 ▪ I Peter 1:17-18 ▪ Titus 2:13-14

Thank God:

Genesis 50:20
You intended to harm me, but God intended it for good to accomplish what is now being done, the saving of many lives.

Psalm 103:1-4
Praise the Lord, my soul; all my inmost being, praise his holy name. Praise the Lord, my soul, and forget not all his benefits—who forgives all your sins and heals all your diseases, who redeems your life from the pit and crowns you with love and compassion...

Romans 6:23
For the wages of sin is death, but the gift of God is eternal life in Christ Jesus our Lord.

Trust God:

Isaiah 43:1
But now, this is what the Lord says—he who created you, Jacob, he who formed you, Israel: "Do not fear, for I have redeemed you; I have summoned you by name; you are mine."

I Peter 1:17-18
Since you call on a Father who judges each person's work impartially, live out your time as foreigners here in reverent fear. For you know that it was not with perishable things such as silver or gold that you were redeemed from the empty way of life handed down to you from your ancestors...

Titus 2:13-14
...while we wait for the blessed hope—the appearing of the glory of our great God and Savior, Jesus Christ, who gave himself for us to redeem us from all wickedness and to purify for himself a people that are his very own, eager to do what is good.

Do not boast about tomorrow, for you do not know what a day will bring forth.

Proverbs 27:1

Do not worry about tomorrow.....each day has enough trouble of its own.

Matthew 6:34

Ask friends about plans for tomorrow, and their answer could be followed by a folksy, Southern colloquial retort...."God willin' and the creek don't rise!" We laugh, but there is surely a kernel of truth in that expression. Only God knows what our tomorrow holds. He warns us not to become puffed up about grandiose plans. And yet God also speaks a gentle "do not worry" to the troubled heart, already dreading tomorrow, afraid more adversity might be coming.

Our God is sovereign over our tomorrows, though we often foolishly picture ourselves in control. Since we know not what a day may bring forth, let us rest on truths from God's word about living today, and trusting Him with tomorrow: *God is able to do immeasurably more than all we ask or imagine. He will keep in perfect peace the mind that is stayed on Him, that trusts in Him.* So read His words and trust His promises. *Be at rest, O my soul, for the Lord has been good to you.* Remember *His mercies are new every morning!* The Lord watches over our coming and going, now and forever. No boasting, no worrying, no borrowing from tomorrow. With conviction, we can always sing out, "Great is your faithfulness," because God will give us "strength for today and bright hope for tomorrow." Each day has its own trouble, but let us fear not for tomorrow because God is already there!

THANK GOD: Isaiah 26:3 ▪ Ephesians 3:20 ▪ Lamentations 3:21-23
TRUST GOD: Psalm 112:7 ▪ Psalm 116:7 ▪ James 4:14-15

Thank God:

Isaiah 26:3
You will keep in perfect peace those whose minds are steadfast, because they trust in you.

Ephesians 3:20
Now to him who is able to do immeasurably more than all we ask or imagine, according to his power that is at work within us...

Lamentations 3:21-23
Yet this I call to mind and therefore I have hope: because of the Lord's great love, we are not consumed, for his compassions never fail. They are new every morning; great is your faithfulness.

Trust God:

Psalm 112:7
They will have no fear of bad news; their hearts are steadfast, trusting in the Lord.

Psalm 116:7
Return to your rest, my soul, for the Lord has been good to you.

James 4:14-15
Why, you do not even know what will happen tomorrow. What is your life? You are a mist that appears for a little while and then vanishes. Instead, you ought to say, "If it is the Lord's will, we will live and do this or that."

....those who hope in the Lord
will renew their strength.
They will soar on wings like eagles;
they will run and not grow
weary, they will walk and not be faint.

Isaiah 40: 31-32

Has a new season of your life brought you to a place of despair or discouragement? Do you identify with a Psalm 42:3 lament: *My tears have been my food day and night, while people say to me all day long, "Where is your God?"* Is it loss of a loved one, an aging issue, a broken relationship, a job loss, pandemic fears, restrictions, new demands at home, a personal set-back? Energy and endurance have vanished into thin air; hopes are fading. Body and mind are weak, weary, and faint.

Words from God are addressed to you in Isaiah 40:28... *Do you not know? Have you not heard? The Lord is the everlasting God, the Creator of the ends of the earth. He will not grow tired or weary, and his understanding no one can fathom. He gives strength to the weary and increases the power of the weak.* Here is hope promised to those who put their trust in the Lord, who seek restoration from weariness and strength for walking, running, even soaring! God knows every detail of your anguish. Wait patiently, reminding yourself of His love and power. Thank Him that He is both willing and able to sustain you in such trying times. Trust Him as you read and reread His words in your Bible; let them secure your hope. Reading is always easier than doing, just as sighing is easier than soaring. But Scripture repeatedly reminds us, *The Lord is good to those whose hope is in Him, to the one who seeks Him.* Be that weary one who knows God's goodness and guidance by seeking His powerful renewal of your hope and strength to walk, run, even soar!!

THANK GOD: Isaiah 41:10 ▪ Lamentations 3:22-23,25 ▪ Nahum 1:7
TRUST GOD: Psalm 57:1-2 ▪ Psalm 119:81-82 ▪ Psalm 143:8

Thank God:

Isaiah 41:10
So do not fear, for I am with you; do not be dismayed, for I am your God. I will strengthen you and help you; I will uphold you with my righteous right hand.

Lamentations 3:22-23, 25
Because of the Lord's great love we are not consumed, for his compassions never fail. They are new every morning; great is your faithfulness.

The Lord is good to those whose hope is in him, to the one who seeks him...

Nahum 1:7
The Lord is good, a refuge in times of trouble. He cares for those who trust in him...

Trust God:

Psalm 57:1-2
Have mercy on me, my God, have mercy on me, for in you I take refuge. I will take refuge in the shadow of your wings until the disaster has passed. I cry out to God Most High, to God, who vindicates me.

Psalm 119:81-82
My soul faints with longing for your salvation, but I have put my hope in your word. My eyes fail, looking for your promise; I say, "When will you comfort me?"

Psalm 143:8
Let the morning bring me word of your unfailing love, for I have put my trust in you. Show me the way I should go, for to you I entrust my life.

Blessed is the man who trusts in the Lord,
whose confidence is in him. He will be
like a tree....

Jeremiah 17:7-8

Our Creator God loves trees! And no wonder! Nothing improves a barren landscape like a few well-placed trees, providing shade, shelter, beauty, fruit, and even the oxygen needed for breathing. Trees became a symbol in Scripture for how the Lord wants His people to live....planted by the waters....flourishing because our roots can reach out to that living water that Jesus alone can supply, so necessary to fruitfulness.

The prophet Jeremiah records the amazing benefits of our being like one of God's trees. Nourished by a stream of water, the tree does not fear when scorching heat comes....its leaves remain green. It has no worries about freshness even in a year of drought, and it never fails to bear fruit. How much am I like (or not) this tree planted by living waters? Am I fearless when the heat of conflict or discouragement tries to scorch my hopes and singe my faith? Do I always stay fresh so I can refresh others, or am I withered or burned out? Am I fretful when a drought of water or resources comes, or do I dig my roots deeper into the Scripture for more living waters of hope? Will I seek to be fruitful even in the worst season of my life by trusting in God's strength, His unfailing love, and His powerful presence? Please, Lord, may I choose wisely!

Every school child reads or learns the final verse of the poem, "Trees" by Joyce Kilmer...."Poems are made by fools like me, but only God can make a tree." And only God can make us like His tree, planted by the river of living water....fearless, fresh, and fruitful.

THANK GOD: Psalm 1:3-4 ▪ Psalm 92:12-14 ▪ Isaiah 61:2-3
TRUST GOD: Psalm 52:8 ▪ Jeremiah 17:8 ▪ John 4:10,14; 15:16

Thank God:

Psalm 1:3-4
That person is like a tree planted by streams of water, which yields its fruit in season and whose leaf does not wither—whatever they do prospers. Not so the wicked! They are like chaff that the wind blows away.

Psalm 92:12-14
The righteous will flourish like a palm tree, they will grow like a cedar of Lebanon; planted in the house of the Lord, they will flourish in the courts of our God. They will still bear fruit in old age, they will stay fresh and green...

Isaiah 61:2-3
...to proclaim the year of the Lord's favor and the day of vengeance of our God, to comfort all who mourn, and provide for those who grieve in Zion—to bestow on them a crown of beauty instead of ashes, the oil of joy instead of mourning, and a garment of praise instead of a spirit of despair. They will be called oaks of righteousness, a planting of the Lord for the display of his splendor.

Trust God:

Psalm 52:8
But I am like an olive tree flourishing in the house of God; I trust in God's unfailing love for ever and ever.

Jeremiah 17:8
They will be like a tree planted by the water that sends out its roots by the stream. It does not fear when heat comes; its leaves are always green. It has no worries in a year of drought and never fails to bear fruit.

John 4:10, 14; 15:16
Jesus answered her, "If you knew the gift of God and who it is that asks you for a drink, you would have asked him and he would have given you living water...

"...whoever drinks the water I give them will never thirst. Indeed, the water I give them will become in them a spring of water welling up to eternal life."

You did not choose me, but I chose you and appointed you so that you might go and bear fruit—fruit that will last—and so that whatever you ask in my name the Father will give you.

Sing to the Lord a new song.... Psalm 98:1
I will sing of the Lord's great love forever....

Psalm 89:1

Sing and make music in your heart to the Lord....

Ephesians 5:19

Hymns and songs are a two-way communication with our Lord. The Scriptures, especially Psalms, are filled with exhortations to bless and praise our God, by singing truths about His love, goodness, justice and mercy. Even if your voice resembles a "joyful noise," God knows you are being obedient to His word. Singing words about God fills our minds and hearts, enriching and confirming truths about Himself and His relationship to us. Never is this more vividly seen than in the singing of Christmas carols. Songs about Jesus' birth will teach both singer and listener who He is, how and why He came, and what our response to Him should be.

Joy to the World: "The Lord has come / Let earth receive her King."

Silent Night: "Son of God, Love's pure light."

Away in a Manger: "The little Lord Jesus lay down his sweet head."

O, Little Town of Bethlehem: "The hopes and fears of all the years are met in thee tonight."

Hark! The Herald Angels Sing: "Glory to the new-born King! Peace on earth and mercy mild, God and sinners reconciled....Hail the heaven-born Prince of Peace, hail the Son of Righteousness....Mild He lays His glory by, born that men no more may die...born to give them second birth....Jesus, our Emmanuel." (God With Us)

O, Holy Night: "....the night of our dear Savior's birth....A thrill of hope, the weary world rejoices....Fall on your knees, hear the angels' voices....O, night divine when Christ was born."

Try using Christmas carols all through the year as a nightly lullaby for small children....your voice, singing about Jesus, can have a calming effect at bedtime, easily followed by prayers of thanksgiving for God's blessings!

THANK GOD: Psalm 100:1-2 KJV ▪ Matthew 1:22 ▪ John 3:3,16
TRUST GOD: Matthew 19:14 ▪ Mark 10:14,16 ▪ Luke 2:9-11

Thank God:

Psalm 100:1-2 KJV
Make a joyful noise unto the Lord, all ye lands. Serve the Lord with gladness: come before his presence with singing.

Matthew 1:22
All this took place to fulfill what the Lord had said through the prophet...

John 3:3, 16
Jesus replied, "Very truly I tell you, no one can see the kingdom of God unless they are born again."

For God so loved the world that he gave his one and only Son, that whoever believes in him shall not perish but have eternal life.

Trust God:

Matthew 19:14
Jesus said, "Let the little children come to me, and do not hinder them, for the kingdom of heaven belongs to such as these."

Mark 10:14, 16
When Jesus saw this, he was indignant. He said to them, "Let the little children come to me, and do not hinder them, for the kingdom of God belongs to such as these."

And he took the children in his arms, placed his hands on them and blessed them.

Luke 2:9-11
An angel of the Lord appeared to them, and the glory of the Lord shone around them, and they were terrified. But the angel said to them, "Do not be afraid. I bring you good news that will cause great joy for all the people. Today in the town of David a Savior has been born to you; he is the Messiah, the Lord.

....do not worry about what to say or how to say it. At that time you will be given what to say....

Matthew 10:19

Few things are more terrifying than speaking out in a hostile setting. Sweaty palms, a racing heart, and butterflies churning in the pits of our stomachs reveal anxieties about performance, perfection, and personal acceptance. Even if we have prayed and thoroughly prepared, we can still feel inadequate or unworthy, thinking someone else could do or say it better. God's word says be not anxious about anything. Not even speaking up in public? Not even then....*but in everything by prayer and petition, with thanksgiving, present your requests to God.*

Moses had to be assured God would help him speak and teach him what to say in leading Israel. (Exodus 4:11) When Jesus sent His disciples out to teach and heal, He gave them the instructions in advance, knowing human nature to be fearful of speaking out in God's name. Jesus was preparing them for far more scary situations than anything you or I might ever expect to face: arrest, flogging, trials. Jesus said, "at that time" the words would be given to speak. Their obedient actions would precede the Spirit-prompted words needed for those moments.

God-given words spoken with a trusting heart attitude and a clear conscience become effective face-to-face communication. You and I may not be called on to speak out in the same hostile arena as Christian faith pioneers. But if ever we are, take heart and give thanks! We, too, can trust God to supply us at just the right time with His words and His way of speaking them fearlessly.

THANK GOD: Colossians 3:16 ▪ Luke 12:11-12 ▪ Ephesians 4:15
TRUST GOD: Psalm 19:14 ▪ Deuteronomy 11:18 ▪ Philippians 4:6-7

Thank God:

Colossians 3:16
Let the message of Christ dwell among you richly as you teach and admonish one another with all wisdom through psalms, hymns, and songs from the Spirit, singing to God with gratitude in your hearts.

Luke 12:11-12
When you are brought before synagogues, rulers and authorities, do not worry about how you will defend yourselves or what you will say, for the Holy Spirit will teach you at that time what you should say.

Ephesians 4:15
Instead, speaking the truth in love, we will grow to become in every respect the mature body of him who is the head, that is, Christ.

Trust God:

Psalm 19:14
May these words of my mouth and this meditation of my heart be pleasing in your sight, Lord, my Rock and my Redeemer.

Deuteronomy 11:18
Fix these words of mine in your hearts and minds; tie them as symbols on your hands and bind them on your foreheads.

Philippians 4:6-7
Do not be anxious about anything, but in every situation, by prayer and petition, with thanksgiving, present your requests to God. And the peace of God, which transcends all understanding, will guard your hearts and your minds in Christ Jesus.

*Be joyful in hope, patient in affliction,
faithful in prayer.*

Romans 12:12

This concise, ten-word summary of a God-pleasing inner life brings to mind wise words from Susanna Wesley, early 18th century Christian wife and mother: "There are two things to do about the Gospel. Believe it and behave it." First, we <u>believe</u> Christ died for our sin and was raised to life, assuring us of eternity with Him. Responding to the Gospel by faith, we gratefully seek the Spirit's help to <u>behave</u> according to God's word and ways....both to please Him and to witness to His goodness.

Be joyful in hope. God's desire is for His own to have joy in the hoping process, whether going through trials and suffering or awaiting Christ's return. *May the God of Hope fill you with all joy and peace in believing.*...How like God to give joy and peace to the hopes we have entrusted to Him! Even if hope falters, ask for His joy and peace.

Be *patient in affliction.* Trials are common to all mankind, but reactions to them vary. We pray for speedy healing and rapid dealing with personal or familial troubles. But God is rarely hurried, and patience is an attribute He seeks to develop in us. Trust His timing.

Be *faithful in prayer.* The high privilege of knowing God is the invitation to commune with Him in personal prayer. Scripture advises us to pray for one another, to pray without ceasing, to pray with thanks in desperate times and in joyful times. Persevere in prayer. God is there, and He hears and cares. Hallelujah! Behave the Gospel of Jesus: choose to be joyful in hope, patient in affliction, faithful in prayer.

THANK GOD: Romans 15:13 ▪ Galatians 5:22 ESV ▪ James 1:2-4
TRUST GOD: Romans 5:1-5 ▪ Philippians 4:6 ▪ Hebrews 11:6

Thank God:

Romans 15:13
May the God of hope fill you with all joy and peace as you trust in him, so that you may overflow with hope by the power of the Holy Spirit.

Galatians 5:22 ESV
But the fruit of the Spirit is love, joy, peace, patience, kindness, goodness, faithfulness...

James 1:2-4
Consider it pure joy, my brothers and sisters, whenever you face trials of many kinds, because you know that the testing of your faith produces perseverance. Let perseverance finish its work so that you may be mature and complete, not lacking anything.

Trust God:

Romans 5:1-5
Therefore, since we have been justified through faith, we have peace with God through our Lord Jesus Christ, through whom we have gained access by faith into this grace in which we now stand. And we boast in the hope of the glory of God. Not only so, but we also glory in our sufferings, because we know that suffering produces perseverance; perseverance, character; and character, hope. And hope does not put us to shame, because God's love has been poured out into our hearts through the Holy Spirit, who has been given to us.

Philippians 4:6
Do not be anxious about anything, but in every situation, by prayer and petition, with thanksgiving, present your requests to God.

Hebrews 11:6
And without faith it is impossible to please God, because anyone who comes to him must believe that he exists and that he rewards those who earnestly seek him.

(Jesus) replied, "My mother and my brothers
are those who hear God's word and
put it into practice."

Luke 8:21

Whether you are learning to play a sport or a musical instrument, or memorizing the lines of a play or a favorite Psalm, the "PMP" maxim always applies....Practice Makes Perfect. This precept is no less true about living Biblically in day-to-day life. Jesus reveals His family seeks to do just that. The <u>action</u> words of the Scriptures are easily found....the "doing" verbs. But the <u>attitude</u> adverbs, describing <u>how</u> we do what we do, prompt the need for practice!! God's ways do not naturally come to us, but neither is perfection required. Just seek to please Him by daily putting His word into practice. Here are some of the challenges....one for each day of the month. Let the practicing begin!

Pray thankfully, unceasingly

Sing joyfully	Listen carefully	Sit quietly
Wait patiently	Speak truthfully, kindly	Live simply
Remind gently	Love unconditionally	Work tirelessly
Study diligently	Encourage enthusiastically	Counsel wisely
Act justly	Teach knowledgably	Walk humbly
Respond graciously	Confront fearlessly	Proclaim boldly
Worship reverently	Forgive mercifully	Seek earnestly
Exhort prayerfully	Trust whole-heartedly	Give cheerfully
Rejoice constantly	Share generously	React calmly
Hope expectantly	Witness honestly	Obey faithfully

THANK GOD: II Corinthians 9:11 ▪ Philippians 4:4 ▪ James 1:25
TRUST GOD: Ezekiel 33:31 ▪ Micah 6:8 ▪ Matthew 7:24, 26

Thank God:

II Corinthians 9:11
You will be enriched in every way so that you can be generous on every occasion, and through us your generosity will result in thanksgiving to God.

Philippians 4:4
Rejoice in the Lord always. I will say it again: Rejoice!

James 1:25
But whoever looks intently into the perfect law that gives freedom, and continues in it—not forgetting what they have heard, but doing it—they will be blessed in what they do.

Trust God:

Ezekiel 33:31
My people come to you, as they usually do, and sit before you to hear your words, but they do not put them into practice. Their mouths speak of love, but their hearts are greedy for unjust gain.

Micah 6:8
He has shown you, O mortal, what is good. And what does the Lord require of you? To act justly and to love mercy and to walk humbly with your God.

Matthew 7:24, 26
Therefore everyone who hears these words of mine and puts them into practice is like a wise man who built his house on the rock.

But everyone who hears these words of mine and does not put them into practice is like a foolish man who built his house on sand.

*Those that cling to worthless idols forfeit
the grace that could be theirs.*

Jonah 2:8

Few in the sports world would choose to forfeit a match, a race, or a game. Regret and disappointment are the usual results. Yet we often choose to forgo something far more valuable eternally than an athletic victory. By clinging to worthless idols, visible or invisible, we can forfeit powerful grace that could be ours from the God of all grace.

Warning about idols and idolatry is a long chapter in God's training and maturing His chosen people. Israel was commanded by God to have no other gods before the Lord God Almighty....to worship nothing and no one except Him. Today's "worthless idols," rarely handmade, are often invisible, but can be a consuming drive for attention or affection. Power, fitness, success, beauty, possessions, personal preferences, style ....none inherently wrong....unless they become our life-center, instead of Almighty God. Think your happiness is shortchanged by obedience? Or that God's call jeopardizes your future? Better check with Jonah.

Runaway prophet Jonah heard God's call to preach repentance to pagan Nineveh, but he fled in the opposite direction. Were his idols stubborn pride, exclusiveness, hate for an enemy, his comfort zone? Praying from the belly of a great fish, seaweed round his head, Jonah had to admit idols are a grace-preventer....and he surely needed God's redeeming, saving grace at that moment! Rescued from the deep to obey God's calling, Jonah gave thanks for life-saving grace. God's mercy and grace finally convicted Jonah, and Nineveh's repentance came with his obedience to God's second call. Forfeit idols, not His merciful grace!

THANK GOD: Exodus 20:2-3 ▪ Jonah 2:9-10 ▪ II Corinthians 9:8
TRUST GOD: Jonah 2:5-7 ▪ I Peter 5:10 ▪ I Timothy 1:12-14

Thank God:

Exodus 20:2-3
I am the Lord your God, who brought you out of Egypt, out of the land of slavery. You shall have no other gods before me.

Jonah 2:9-10
"But I, with shouts of grateful praise, will sacrifice to you. What I have vowed I will make good. I will say, 'Salvation comes from the Lord.'" And the Lord commanded the fish, and it vomited Jonah onto dry land.

II Corinthians 9:8
And God is able to make all grace abound to you, so that in all things at all times, having all that you need, you will abound in every good work.

Trust God:

Jonah 2:5-7
The engulfing waters threatened me, the deep surrounded me; seaweed was wrapped around my head. To the roots of the mountains I sank down; the earth beneath barred me in forever. But you, Lord my God, brought my life up from the pit. When my life was ebbing away, I remembered you, Lord, and my prayer rose to you, to your holy temple.

I Peter 5:10
And the God of all grace, who called you to his eternal glory in Christ, after you have suffered a little while, will himself restore you and make you strong, firm and steadfast.

I Timothy 1:12-14
I thank Christ Jesus our Lord, who has given me strength, that he considered me trustworthy, appointing me to his service. Even though I was once a blasphemer and a persecutor and a violent man, I was shown mercy because I acted in ignorance and unbelief. The grace of our Lord was poured out on me abundantly, along with the faith and love that are in Christ Jesus.

Be strong and courageous ....

Joshua 1:6-7

After Moses died, having passed the baton of leadership to Joshua, God sought to reassure His younger servant. The Israelites were on the brink of entering the land promised to them by God years before. But how could Joshua ever step into the leadership shoes of Moses? Only by hearing multiple times from God that He would be with him just as He had been with Moses. And further, God repeatedly told Joshua to *be strong and courageous.* Do you ever hear a Bible verse or phrase repeated to you several times in a day in different contexts: on the radio or TV, from a song or a friend, or during a devotional time? Grab hold of it, meditate on it, see how it could be a needed word of encouragement from the Lord for you to become something you are not (yet).

"O Lord, please forgive me when I fail to believe and take to heart your words of assurance and promise. In facing every challenge, may I become stronger and more courageous....able to trust you rather than pout fearfully, to thank you rather than complain and criticize, to remember all the times and ways your faithfulness has blessed and rescued me. If I am feeling alone, weak, useless, helpless, hopeless, frail, or fearful, teach me once more that your *grace is sufficient* for my every need. With each crisis of confidence may I, somehow, hear these words said to your chosen ones: *Do not be dismayed, for I am your God. I will strengthen you and help you; I will uphold you with my righteous right hand.* (Isaiah 41:10) Joshua became your strong and courageous leader....enable me to stand firm in the truth of your Word." Amen!

THANK GOD: Nehemiah 8:10 ▪ Psalm 18:1 ▪ I Corinthians 16:13
TRUST GOD: Deuteronomy 31:6-8 ▪ Joshua 1:9 ▪ II Corinthians 12:9

Thank God:

Nehemiah 8:10
Nehemiah said, "Go and enjoy choice food and sweet drinks, and send some to those who have nothing prepared. This day is holy to our Lord. Do not grieve, for the joy of the Lord is your strength."

Psalm 18:1
I love you, Lord, my strength.

I Corinthians 16:13
Be on your guard; stand firm in the faith; be courageous; be strong.

Trust God:

Deuteronomy 31:6-8
Be strong and courageous. Do not be afraid or terrified because of them, for the Lord your God goes with you; he will never leave you nor forsake you. Then Moses summoned Joshua and said to him in the presence of all Israel, "Be strong and courageous, for you must go with this people into the land that the Lord swore to their ancestors to give them, and you must divide it among them as their inheritance. The Lord himself goes before you and will be with you; he will never leave you nor forsake you. Do not be afraid; do not be discouraged."

Joshua 1:9
Have I not commanded you? Be strong and courageous. Do not be afraid; do not be discouraged, for the Lord your God will be with you wherever you go.

II Corinthians 12:9
But he said to me, "My grace is sufficient for you, for my power is made perfect in weakness." Therefore I will boast all the more gladly about my weaknesses, so that Christ's power may rest on me.

Worthy is the Lamb, who was slain, to receive power and wealth, wisdom and strength and honor and glory and praise.

Revelation 5:12

Classical music lovers will recognize this powerful chorale from Handel's The Messiah. Heart-stirring music is a gift, but the words are not Handel's....they are God's words in the Bible about Jesus at the end of the age. Jesus, the Lamb of God, is surrounded by a multitude of angels proclaiming the triumph of His sacrificial death, glorious resurrection, and His worthiness to reign. Could I make the same proclamation in thanks for His dying in my place to ensure me abundant and eternal life?

How could I give Jesus power? By surrendering control of my life to Him, letting go of any desire for self-sufficiency or self-sovereignty. What wealth could I give to the Creator of all things in heaven and earth? As the little shepherd boy said, "I could give Him my heart"....in love, in thanks, in generosity, in humble joy. The ultimate source of all wisdom invites me to ask Him for it. I can seek His words in Scripture, then ask Him for a desire to live by them. Applying God's word to life offers a glimpse of His wisdom to a watching, wondering world.

Giving God strength is only possible when I acknowledge my weakness, remembering His words, *My strength is made perfect in weakness*....so when I am weak, then I am strong in the Lord and the power of His might. To give honor to God, I revere with awe His place as Sovereign Lord and Judge of all the earth. Even when no one sees, I will exercise integrity. I can give God glory when I praise Him with words of love, a thankful heart, and a desire to please Him in every area of life.

THANK GOD: II Corinthians 12:9 ▪ James 1:5-6 ▪ Revelation 4:11, 5:9
TRUST GOD: Psalm 71:14 ▪ Proverbs 3:9-10 ▪ Ephesians 1:18-20

Thank God:

II Corinthians 12:9
But he said to me, "My grace is sufficient for you, for my power is made perfect in weakness." Therefore I will boast all the more gladly about my weaknesses, so that Christ's power may rest on me.

James 1:5-6
If any of you lacks wisdom, you should ask God, who gives generously to all without finding fault, and it will be given to you. But when you ask, you must believe and not doubt, because the one who doubts is like a wave of the sea, blown and tossed by the wind.

Revelation 4:11, 5:9
You are worthy, our Lord and God, to receive glory and honor and power, for you created all things, and by your will they were created and have their being.

And they sang a new song, saying: "You are worthy to take the scroll and to open its seals, because you were slain, and with your blood you purchased for God persons from every tribe and language and people and nation."

Trust God:

Psalm 71:14
As for me, I will always have hope; I will praise you more and more.

Proverbs 3:9-10
Honor the Lord with your wealth, with the first fruits of all your crops; then your barns will be filled to overflowing, and your vats will brim over with new wine.

Ephesians 1:18-20
I pray that the eyes of your heart may be enlightened in order that you may know the hope to which he has called you, the riches of his glorious inheritance in his holy people, and his incomparably great power for us who believe. That power is the same as the mighty strength he exerted when he raised Christ from the dead and seated him at his right hand in the heavenly realms...

*The memory of the righteous will
be a blessing....*

Proverbs 10:7

Have you ever left a funeral service wondering what might one day be said about you in recognition, remembrance or appreciation? It is challenging to think about leaving a legacy, especially one that can outlive you. Fame or power might mean a building, a ship, or a bridge is named after you. Generous philanthropy to non-profits is a noteworthy and noble legacy, helping make life better for many. Foundations and endowed scholarships benefit and prepare the next generation for service or livelihood. Seek God's direction in giving your time and assets on behalf of others, even if you may not live to see the fruition of your impact or influence. Hope always is to help and bless another.

But be not discouraged if you are unable to leave any tangible or visible evidence of your life or work. Proverbs 22:1 tells us *a good name is more desirable than great riches; to be esteemed is better than silver or gold.* God values your integrity and character more than achievements. In adversity or prosperity, what we <u>are</u> has eternal consequences and is more important than what we possess or <u>do</u>. Your memory will be a blessing because of who you <u>are</u>! One obituary thanked the deceased for ways he personally blessed his associates....allowing common people to do uncommon things and showing them an enduring legacy of integrity. What will your legacy be? Love? Hope? Faith? Generosity? Grace? Courage? Prayer? Only time will tell.

THANK GOD: Psalm 112:5-6 ▪ Psalm 147:10-11 ▪ Matthew 26:12-13
TRUST GOD: Proverbs 22:9 ▪ I Thessalonians 1:2 ▪ Romans 1:16-17

Thank God:

Psalm 112:5-6
Good will come to those who are generous and lend freely, who conduct their affairs with justice. Surely the righteous will never be shaken; they will be remembered forever.

Psalm 147:10-11
His pleasure is not in the strength of the horse, nor his delight in the legs of the warrior; the Lord delights in those who fear him, who put their hope in his unfailing love.

Matthew 26:12-13
When she poured this perfume on my body, she did it to prepare me for burial. Truly I tell you, wherever this gospel is preached throughout the world, what she has done will also be told, in memory of her.

Trust God:

Proverbs 22:9
The generous will themselves be blessed, for they share their food with the poor.

I Thessalonians 1:2
We always thank God for all of you and continually mention you in our prayers.

Romans 1:16-17
For I am not ashamed of the gospel, because it is the power of God that brings salvation to everyone who believes: first to the Jew, then to the Gentile. For in the gospel the righteousness of God is revealed—a righteousness that is by faith from first to last, just as it is written: "The righteous will live by faith."

Be joyful always; pray continually; give thanks in all circumstances. For this is God's will for you in Christ Jesus.

I Thessalonians 5:16-18

Did you know the Scripture calls you to multitasking? How else could you fulfill the admonitions to "be joyful always," to "pray continually," and always to "give thanks"? Is that even possible? Joyfulness is a matter of the heart, not of current circumstances. When Christ reigns and rules in your heart, joy is the result. From the Bible you learn God loves you, is with you, can use every situation in your life for good somehow, and promises you eternal life with Him. Joy is a hallmark of Christianity, a fruit of the indwelling Holy Spirit; it cannot be manufactured or faked in a momentary happiness.

Even if you are full of joy, how can you pray continually? God has promised His presence is always with us, so we can be in constant communication with Him....that is what prayer is. We can pray while we are walking, driving, riding, standing, sitting, studying, or resting. Continual prayer is simply ongoing communication. Silently or verbally, eyes open or shut, we can acknowledge to God our needs, mistakes, failures, sorrows, hopes, delights. Then we listen, anticipating a response from Him in that still small voice in our minds and hearts.

God's unfailing love and faithfulness means we can always give thanks, even when our situation seems totally to the contrary. In Christ Jesus, we have the power to be joyful, prayerful, and thankful all at once. May these three traits so mark your life that others are blessed!

THANK GOD: Romans 8:28 ▪ Ephesians 5:20 ▪ Philippians 4:4
TRUST GOD: Nehemiah 8:10 ▪ Habakkuk 3:17-18 ▪ Luke 18:1

Thank God:

Romans 8:28
And we know that in all things God works for the good of those who love him, who have been called according to his purpose.

Ephesians 5:20
...always giving thanks to God the Father for everything, in the name of our Lord Jesus Christ.

Philippians 4:4
Rejoice in the Lord always. I will say it again: Rejoice!

Trust God:

Nehemiah 8:10
Nehemiah said, "Go and enjoy choice food and sweet drinks, and send some to those who have nothing prepared. This day is holy to our Lord. Do not grieve, for the joy of the Lord is your strength."

Habakkuk 3:17-18
Though the fig tree does not bud and there are no grapes on the vines, though the olive crop fails and the fields produce no food, though there are no sheep in the pen and no cattle in the stalls, yet I will rejoice in the Lord, I will be joyful in God my Savior.

Luke 18:1
Then Jesus told his disciples a parable to show them that they should always pray and not give up.

*.....weeping may endure for a night, but
joy comes in the morning.*

Psalm 30:5b KJV

Do you ever feel as if you are in the "night" of your life....not just half of a 24-hour cycle, but on a bed of personal sorrow, in the darkness of the unknown, with a heartbreak or great loss? Does "strength for today and bright hope for tomorrow" sound like a pipe dream rather than a song lyric? Fear not! Though it may seem as if the shade has been pulled down on your window of hope, our God is known for some amazing promises to His people in their dark nights of the soul.

The God of Hope is also the God of exchanges and replacements. In Jeremiah, He promises, *I will turn their mourning into gladness; I will give them comfort and joy instead of sorrow.* (31:13) Through Isaiah, God speaks to the grieving in Zion about bestowing on them *a crown of beauty instead of ashes, the oil of gladness instead of mourning, and a garment of praise, instead of a spirit of despair.* (61:3) We can use these very words in prayer to God, asking Him to give us these exchanges. Remember that every morning His mercies are new, so thank Him for His faithfulness as you ask for and await an exchange.

Consider another dimension of being in the night of your life: think of the sorrow, the pain Christ bore....the burden of the Cross, dying in our place, to secure our eternal destiny with Him. Whatever your loss or sorrow, cry out to Jesus who has borne it with you. Entrust yourself to His peace and comfort. Look for a great exchange to start bringing you out of the night into a day of joy and hope and praise.

THANK GOD: Lamentations 3:22-23 ▪ Psalm 18:28 ▪ Hebrews 12:2
TRUST GOD: Psalm 42:5,8-11 ▪ Psalm 30:11-12 ▪ Philippians 4:6-7

Thank God:

Lamentations 3:22-23
Because of the Lord's great love we are not consumed, for his compassions never fail. They are new every morning; great is your faithfulness.

Psalm 18:28
You, Lord, keep my lamp burning; my God turns my darkness into light.

Hebrews 12:2
...fixing our eyes on Jesus, the pioneer and perfecter of faith. For the joy set before him he endured the cross, scorning its shame, and sat down at the right hand of the throne of God.

Trust God:

Psalm 42:5, 8-11
Why, my soul, are you downcast? Why so disturbed within me? Put your hope in God, for I will yet praise him, my Savior and my God.

By day the Lord directs his love, at night his song is with me—a prayer to the God of my life. I say to God my Rock, "Why have you forgotten me? Why must I go about mourning, oppressed by the enemy?" My bones suffer mortal agony as my foes taunt me, saying to me all day long, "Where is your God?" Why, my soul, are you downcast? Why so disturbed within me? Put your hope in God, for I will yet praise him, my Savior and my God.

Psalm 30:11-12
You turned my wailing into dancing; you removed my sackcloth and clothed me with joy, that my heart may sing your praises and not be silent. Lord my God, I will praise you forever.

Philippians 4:6-7
Do not be anxious about anything, but in every situation, by prayer and petition, with thanksgiving, present your requests to God. And the peace of God, which transcends all understanding, will guard your hearts and your minds in Christ Jesus.

Now unto him who is able to do
immeasurably more
than all we ask or imagine,
according to his power that
is at work within us....to him be glory....

Ephesians 3:20

A faltering faith, a flickering hope need only meditate on this declaration of God's power and goodness to begin to trust Him anew.

Able to do immeasurably more than all we ask or imagine indicates there is no limit to what God can or will do on our behalf when we seek Him with all our heart. Every perfect gift our heavenly Father provides for His children can be related to a "more than" connection.

God is love. The love He gives us is more than a sometimes love. It is an unfailing love, an unconditional love, an everlasting love! His desire is that we know the width, length, height, and depth of this love in Christ Jesus, His Son. Then God invites us to come with confidence into His throne room where we can receive mercy and find grace....an endless mercy, new every morning, and an abounding grace, not given begrudgingly, but freely. The God of hope fills us with joy and peace in trusting Him. The hope He gives is more than a faint glimmer; it is an overflowing hope that cannot be hidden....and begs to be shared.

When we begin to see the "more than all we ask or imagine" aspect of God's gracious goodness, we should not be surprised to witness daily miracles and wonders from His hand....perfect timing for small tasks; unexpected, joyful encounters; and amazing energy. Even Job knew God performs *wonders that cannot be fathomed, miracles that cannot be counted.* Are you watching for countless wonders in your life situation? Ask God for spiritual sight to behold more than the eye can see!

THANK GOD: Job 9:10 ▪ Exodus 15:11, 13 ▪ Romans 15:13
TRUST GOD: Psalm 33:20-22 ▪ Ephesians 3:17-19 ▪ Hebrews 4:16

Thank God:

Job 9:10
He performs wonders that cannot be fathomed, miracles that cannot be counted.

Exodus 15:11, 13
Who among the gods is like you, Lord? Who is like you—majestic in holiness, awesome in glory, working wonders?

In your unfailing love you will lead the people you have redeemed. In your strength you will guide them to your holy dwelling.

Romans 15:13
May the God of hope fill you with all joy and peace as you trust in him, so that you may overflow with hope by the power of the Holy Spirit.

Trust God:

Psalm 33:20-22
We wait in hope for the Lord; he is our help and our shield. In him our hearts rejoice, for we trust in his holy name. May your unfailing love be with us, Lord, even as we put our hope in you.

Ephesians 3:17-19
...so that Christ may dwell in your hearts through faith. And I pray that you, being rooted and established in love, may have power, together with all the Lord's holy people, to grasp how wide and long and high and deep is the love of Christ, and to know this love that surpasses knowledge—that you may be filled to the measure of all the fullness of God.

Hebrews 4:16
Let us then approach God's throne of grace with confidence, so that we may receive mercy and find grace to help us in our time of need.

EPILOGUE

That God is always better than we know was forever reinforced in my life when the lockdowns for the coronavirus pandemic were put in place. The long, terrifying, and frustrating days of grim news and loss quickly began to dash my hopes and ignite my fears that life, as I had known it, might never return. I was at a point of needing to revise and finalize pages for <u>Windows of Hope</u>. Who but God could create a silver lining for those scary days and simultaneously re-energize a calling, using His words of Hope to encourage my own despairing heart once again? Great is His faithfulness!

God's words began to flow together like a Thanksgiving holiday recipe, always prompting my Thanks and Trust in Him:

> *My God shall supply all of my needs according to his riches in Christ Jesus. In His great mercy He has given us new birth into a living hope through the resurrection of Jesus Christ from the dead....*

> *Let us then approach the throne of grace with confidence, so that we may receive mercy and find grace to help in our time of need. By prayer and petition, with thanksgiving, let your requests be known unto God. With God, all things are possible.... [He] will never leave you or forsake you. God is able to work all things together for good to those who love him and are called, according to his purpose. In this world you will have trouble. But take heart (KJV "be of good cheer"), I have overcome the world.***

The COVID-19 pandemic created more trouble and tribulation than the world has known in the past one hundred years. The life of every man, woman and child on earth has been touched in some way by the lethal power of the virus to kill and to destroy both sacred and routine patterns of life. Hopelessness has abounded. Few have been the answers to questions regarding losses of life and livelihood. Yet each day we can choose to call upon a Sovereign Lord, in thanks and trust, to give strength, wisdom, and grace. The God of Hope can even give our hearts joy and peace when we hold fast to His outstretched arm and unfailing love….and let the Holy Spirit empower us to abound in Hope.

** Scriptures in this paragraph are from Philippians 4:6,19, I Peter 1:3, Hebrews 4:16, Joshua 1:5, Matthew 19:26, Romans 8:28, and John 16:33.

ACKNOWLEDGMENTS

More gratitude than I can express belongs to my daughter, Lynn Turpin Hendricks, for the multitude of ways she made <u>Windows of Hope</u> a reality. Her superior computer skills, the time spent recording and proofreading Scripture passages and messages, and her strategizing for the overall layout of the book were the keys to its completion. My son-in-law, Bill Hendricks, a seasoned Christian author himself, lent encouragement and inspiration. (Bill wrote multiple books in the years it took for this one to come together.) Dr. Brittany Hendricks Faske served as our copy edtior and proofreader. Her talents and keen eyes suited our editing needs perfectly.

Many thanks go to our talented and very helpful publisher, Lawrence Luby, of HIS Publishing Group, who was creative, patient, and adaptive to our questions and requests. He oversaw the creation of the cover, finding an artist who could put the vision for a *Window of Hope* on paper in vivid color.

My family has always been, and will forever be, a constant source of joy, blessing, and support. My husband and I had the pleasure of living most of our lives in our hometown. I am thankful that at one time four generations of the family were able to interact with each other in various ways and places, remembering each other's life stories, celebrating different occasions, or grieving losses together. Whether playing with our darling grandchildren (now in college), enjoying our grown-up son and daughter, or helping parents and grandparents in the golden years, many were the opportunities and moments to Thank and Trust our Sovereign God! Great is His faithfulness!